confessions of a slacker wife

Praise for Muffy Mead-Ferro's
confessions of a slacker mom

"The author's extra-dry Wyoming sarcasm ... puts New Yorkers to shame."

—*Los Angeles Times*

"*Confessions of a Slacker Mom* has plenty of insight on raising kids without succumbing to the pressure and guilt of modern middle-class parenting. This quick, entertaining read provides welcome validation for the feet-on-the-couch mom many of us long to be."

—*Chicago Tribune*

"A welcome relief from the flood of how-to-mother-perfectly tomes, Mead-Ferro's short and sweet book is a reminder not to take parenthood too seriously."

—*Publisher's Weekly*

"Mead-Ferro might sound callous if it weren't for her wicked sense of humor."

—*The Washington Post*

"A brief, breezy take on a theme that seems to be resonating with a lot of mothers right now."

—*USA Today*

"A humorous and candid look at how one woman learned to stop feeling guilty and embrace being an imperfect mother."

—*Child*

"If you feel guilty about the fact that you want a life outside your kids, that your child isn't yet on the Ivy League fast track, or that you haven't protected her from every last bump and bruise—don't. Read Muffy Mead-Ferro's hilarious *Confessions of a Slacker Mom* and you'll realize you're doing a pretty good job."

—*HealthyFamily*

"No matter which parenting books my customers choose, I will insist this book be at the top of their list."

—Philip Prock, Bookseller, Books Inc., San Francisco, CA

"Laugh out loud funny! Someone has finally told it like it should be with parenting and children."

—Lee Musgjerd, Lee's Book Emporium, Glasgow, Montana

confessions of a slacker wife

Muffy Mead-Ferro

Da Capo

LIFE
LONG

A Member of the
Perseus Books Group

Set in Kennerly_ 11 on 17 by the Perseus Books Group

Library of Congress Cataloging-in-Publication Data

Mead-Ferro, Muffy.
  Confessions of a slacker wife / Muffy Mead-Ferro.– 1st Da Capo Press ed.
    p. cm.
  Includes bibliographical references and index.
  ISBN 0-7382-1016-1 (pbk. : alk. paper)
  1. Wives–United States. 2. Marriage–United States. 3. Wives–Humor.
  4. Mead-Ferro, Muffy. 5. Wives–United States–Biography. I. Title.
  HV759.M42 2005
  306.872'3–dc22

                                    2005002731

First Da Capo Press edition 2005

Published by Da Capo Press
A Member of the Perseus Books Group
www.dacapopress.com

Da Capo Press books are available at special discounts for bulk purchases in the U.S. by corporations, institutions, and other organizations. For more information, please contact the Special Markets Department at the Perseus Books Group, 11 Cambridge Center, Cambridge, MA 02142, or call (800) 255-1514 or (617) 252-5298, or e-mail special.markets@perseusbooks.com.

1 2 3 4 5 6 7 8 9—08 07 06 05

For my husband

TABLE OF CONTENTS

———◆———

chapter 1

Meet the Mrs.

– 1 –

Maybe once a week a piece of mail gets pushed through the slot in our front door addressed to Mr. and Mrs. Michael A. Ferro. I've been married for eight years, but it always takes me a second to comprehend the fact that my name is on the envelope. Yes . . . there it is right there, in all its glory: Mrs.

Oh, I know. Whoever addressed the envelope was doing it right. They were doing it the way Miss Manners or Emily Post or whoever said to do it, and I'm in favor of good manners. I even like tradition sometimes. In any case, the pieces of correspondence that are addressed that way, such as wedding invitations, are often the epitome of formality and tradition in the first place. So it's no affront to polite society, which I may or may not be a member of, that the address on the envelope follows the customary form as well.

It doesn't bother me anyway. The fact is, I don't think twice about it! It's such a trivial matter in the great scheme of things, and I would hope I have more important things to worry about.

In fact I can't even believe I brought it up, much less started off a book with it. Because, really, this is exactly the sort of insignificant issue that some people love to get caught up in and waste society's time with.

These overly zealous types just love to call people on the carpet for saying words like "Chairman." Now we have to say, "Chair*woman*" or "Chair*person*." These seem awkward, though, so most people I know just use the genderless and personless term "Chair" when speaking about the leader of an organization such as a board of trustees. Or sometimes it's that other disembodied term, "Head." I'm a Head myself for a nonprofit group I've worked with for several years, and it's certainly as grandiose a title as I feel comfortable with. I think I would take Head over Chair, anyway. So I can hardly imagine spending more than one second thinking about the fact that I'm sometimes referred to as Mrs. Michael A. Ferro. Pooh!

Wait, though. Did I say "pooh"? Scratch that. I must admit that I have spent some time thinking about this issue, trying to understand why something so seemingly superficial *would* bother me. As I said, I have more important things to worry about. So why indeed would it irk me in the slightest to be addressed as nothing more than a Mrs., the feminine subclass of my husband, who was known as Mr. Michael A. Ferro before, during, and after I came on the scene, with no adjustment necessary?

But I have now cleverly answered my own question.

It's not just that my husband never has to go by the name of Mr. Muffy Mead, though. The truth is, I don't really feel comfortable being someone who, now that she's married, is known to some people only by her association with a man, the person who presumably heads up the household.

I don't want to sound like I'm overly zealous or anything—dear me, no—but I must admit that sometimes I think about how American women, upon getting married, most often drop their own surname to take that of their husband's. And although I know there are good reasons for doing it, I'm reminded of the fact that African slaves were sometimes given the surnames of their American owners, in an unceremonious dismissal of their own personal histories. So they were known only by their association with the person who was head of the household. The person who, under the laws and customs of the time, owned them. And some of their descendants go by those last names to this day.

Personally, I just can't drum up my enthusiasm for any of the subservient connotations of "wife," no matter what the current customs. I especially don't like feeling subservient to my husband, whom I consider my partner and not the boss-man. That's one of the reasons why, although I'm proud to be married to this man, I'll never deliberately go by the moniker "Mrs. Michael A. Ferro." It's one thing to adopt the family name of Ferro, but I'm just not willing to go by Michael, and I would like to point out to all those people who find great amusement in the name Muffy that at least it fits me better than Mike.

Besides, I have my own personal history. My name was Muffy Mead for thirty-seven years. I'm partial to it. And like so many other women I know, I have accomplished too much under my own banner to simply toss it aside and carry my husband's.

Then again, I did want to adopt my husband's last name when we got married, because it simply makes practical sense for him, for me, and for our two kids to share the same family name. It helps eliminates confusion for sheepheaded institutions such as airlines, insurance companies, and federal governments.

So after some sorting and compiling I arrived at Muffy Mead-Ferro, and I hope it's not too much of an awkward mouthful for those people who already balk at saying things like "Chairperson."

I'm not saying that being a wife in this day and age is tantamount to being a slave or a servant. It used to be so, as we all know, in some cultures at some points in history. And the depressing fact is that it remains so in some parts of the world. But no one I know looks at the wife as her husband's property any more. Women have come a long way in that regard, and hallelujah to that. In the marriages that I admire, the wife is not there to wait on the husband any more than he's there to wait on her.

Not that I never wait on the man. From time to time I really enjoy doing things for my husband, simply as a gesture of affection. And sometimes I even like to do things that involve serving him, quite literally. On the odd Sunday evening, for instance, I might enjoy taking some real trouble to make my husband a special meal, presenting it to him on a tray with his favorite red wine and a set of teeny salt and pepper shakers. But it's my prerogative, not my duty. So maybe the difference between me and the obedient wife of previous generations is that, although I might make the dinner, if my husband ever came home and said, "Why isn't dinner on the table?" I'd probably respond with, "Obviously dear, you haven't cooked it yet."

I hope that doesn't sound bitchy, or even just contrary, because I like being a wife. I especially like being a wife to the particular person I'm married to.

I had a marriage earlier in my life that was short-lived and, fortunately, didn't produce any children. I don't mean to say it was all bad, because it had its good points, one of which was to convince me even more thoroughly that if I ever hooked up with the right guy, I was going to do all I could to make it work. I have a great variety of goals—familial, personal, and professional—but I believe there may be no achievement in my life that counts for more than being happily married.

For one thing, I love my husband. He's smart, funny, kind, and, as far as I'm concerned, exceptionally handsome.

For another thing, my life is immeasurably better since I got married. Now I have someone to help shoulder the responsibilities of life and share in its happiness. Our two children, Belle and Joe, are at the top of both categories, and I hate to even contemplate the idea of being a parent without my husband. I know it can be done, and I know it can be done well, but I'm thankful I don't have to do it.

I'm thankful partly because it's a lot of work and better divided among two people. But I love having someone to share the joy with me, not just the work. My husband is the only other person on earth, for instance, who fully appreciates the comic genius of our children. Our little boy, Joe, still says "cramma" instead of "camera," and we think that's quite funny no matter how many times we hear it, but we don't expect anyone else to laugh.

Besides, I think it's important to Belle and Joe that we have a good relationship. I don't mean a relationship where we don't fight, because we do. We try to stay away from name-calling and hair-pulling, but we do disagree and get mad at each other, and sometimes we even argue strenuously in front of Belle and Joe. We just try to make sure that we resolve things in front of Belle and Joe too. We hope that by providing them with an example of a relationship that's based on love, respect, forgiveness, cooperation, and fun, we'll be setting their expectations high about the kind of relationships they deserve to find for themselves later in their lives.

But being single was very agreeable for both Michael and me, for a long time. We married when he was thirty-six and I was thirty-seven, long enough for us both to have well-established routines as independent single people who were completely in charge of their households, schedules, and bank accounts. This was a level of control that suited us both fine, and that goes double for the bank account.

I can't help but think back fondly to my single days, those days when my house was MY house, my car was MY car, and all

my stuff was mine, mine, mine. Oh! The joy—if only I'd appreciated it at the time—of leaving a magazine on the coffee table,
open to the page I'd been reading, and knowing I'd find it right in
the same spot, open to that same page, a day later! And I still get
the most luxurious, sinful pleasure out of eating crackers and
drinking tea in bed when my husband is out of town, even though
I know I could do it just the same, without being criticized, when
he's home.

There was something wonderful about living alone, and I
know my husband feels the same way. So it hasn't been easy, for
either of us, to accommodate another person who always has
their own pesky ideas about how things should be done.

We've had to work at it. Speaking for myself, I think it's well
worth working at. As much as I always took to living alone, it's
been even more rewarding to be married and to have my own
family. And at the risk of stating the obvious, I want ours to be a
happy family. I want to make my husband happy. I want, in other
words, to be a good wife. But I must admit that during the eight
years we've been married, I've often asked myself, Can I really do
all that I'm apparently supposed to do to be a good wife?

It's different for my generation than it was for generations
past, in ways that are far more substantial than whether or not

we take our husbands' last names. For one thing, women's lives have changed radically in the past couple of generations because so many of us are working full or part time outside our homes. So we're out there taking care of bosses, clients, and customers.

But too often, when we get home, it feels like we're supposed to take care of everything there too. Although so many of us have entered the work force, we've been unable to shed—or share—so many of the duties that were keeping us busy full-time *before* we had outside jobs. Doing it all makes me feel like I'm tearing along on a treadmill that doesn't ever get turned off, where the slightest misstep will lead to a very undignified crash. This is tiring. This makes me jumpy and irritable. Maybe even unreasonable.

Case in point: My husband exasperates me sorely from time to time by asking such questions as "Do we have bread?"

I realize from an intellectual standpoint that this is nothing to get irked about. I am aware that from my husband's straightforward viewpoint, "Do we have bread?" is a yes-or-no question as to the status of a simple material fact. "Do we have bread?" does not, in his mind, warrant a reply such as the following from me:

"*Do we have bread?* Am I to understand, from your question, that you are saying you do not know after the five-and-a-half years we have spent in this house where the bread is kept? Or should I simply infer that you are too lazy to look in the bread basket? And is it also the case, since you would never be expected to keep abreast of what the bread supply is or, God forbid, actually go to the store to replace the bread that we've eaten or let get moldy, that it is my job and my job alone to know what the bread inventory is and to do what's necessary to make sure it is maintained at a level where you can eat bread whenever you feel like it? Or is this just your irritatingly indirect way of asking me to get up and get you a piece of bread?"

Not that I would ever, ever let loose with that kind of a sarcastic diatribe. Besides, if I did, the only point it would make with my husband would be that I was grouchy. And he'd be right. But sometimes I do feel grouchy. Because keeping us supplied with groceries is just one of the many thankless if not completely invisible chores that it seems I have on my list simply because I am the wife.

"When can I get my own wife?" I've often wondered aloud. I've needed one since before I was one.

I remember the first time I decided that what I really needed to get ahead in my profession was a wife. And now I am talking about the subservient connotations of "wife." Connotations which, I must admit, aren't nearly so offensive when one is the serv*ee* rather than the serv*er*.

I was working at an advertising agency, always operating under an unreasonable deadline set by someone who seemed to have no concept of the work involved. I was not only coming up with ad ideas at a pace that could never be justified—unless you watch TV and have witnessed firsthand how, in our advanced society, we have an insatiable need for a continuous incoming stream of new commercials at all times—but I was also in management. I was the only woman on our company's executive committee, a particularly competitive setting. I was putting in fifty to sixty hours a week on a regular basis and traveling three or four times a month.

I wasn't complaining about that, though, because everyone around me was doing the same thing. The difference was that most of my peers were married men with stay-at-home wives. So although we were all working long hours, they, unlike me, had someone at home doing *everything else.* Picking up the dry cleaning. Going to the grocery store. Paying the bills. Doing the laundry. Sending gifts and thank you notes. Keeping the house clean. Shuttling the kids.

So of course my male colleagues could go into the office on Saturdays. And Sundays, if someone suggested it. What the heck! Let's schedule all our meetings to occur out-of-state, too, while we're at it—it doesn't matter!

That's why I often thought to myself, If I really want to compete with these guys, and still get at least seven hours of sleep a
night, I need a wife. At that time I was single, but even then I had
many more things to take care of outside the office than my male
counterparts. And now that I'm married with children, my
domestic chores have increased a hundred-fold.

Also, now that I'm a wife and mother, I realize looking back
that those stay-at-home wives, the ones doing *everything else* for
the men I was working with, had even more on their plates than
their husbands did. The number of things the wives had to do
couldn't even be contemplated within a fifty- or sixty-hour work-
week. Their chores were the gift that kept on giving, long after
their husbands were off the clock.

But it's not just the number of wifely chores I have—and
the fact that I don't have my own wife to unload them on— that
chafes me. It's also the "invisible" nature of my household tasks
that makes them a little more onerous. Of course, it's only rea-
sonable for the workload in any operation, including a
household, to be divided according to who does what best, and
I'm in favor of that. Even if it means the work ends up being
divided along somewhat traditional, what some people would
call sexist, lines.

The fact is, my husband is far better at hanging light fixtures, and I'm far better at folding laundry. But for some diabolical reason it seems that most of our chores pan out that way—they happen to divide up along lines of gender. What's more galling, though, is that seems to so often make them unequal in terms of their visibility.

You hang a light fixture and it's up there for everyone to see. "Wow, that looks great," I can be expected to declare before my husband is finished putting the last screw in the ceiling plate. And even other people, when they visit our dining room a week later, might say, "Hey, you got a new chandelier." That sort of recognition is kind of a nice payoff for the person who hung the light fixture. Or planted the tree. Or built the fence. Or installed the new stereo. It would tend to make that person feel like they were valued and appreciated. That, I can only imagine, must be nice.

But who's there to say how well my husband's clean underwear were folded? Do the dinner guests, a week later, remark on it? No. The symmetry, consistency, and precision with which I can fold and stack a half-dozen pairs of boxer shorts is completely lost on the person who unfolds them, so it's hardly surprising if the people who came over to eat dinner don't take notice.

I don't have that expectation of visitors, though, so please don't be nervous if you ever end up being a guest in our home. I'm just comparing my chores to my husband's in terms of their visibility to my family members.

The only encounter my family members have with laundry is in their creation of it, a trick they perform merely by removing clothes from their bodies. A shirt, as it passes over the person's neck and ears, no matter how short a time it's been worn or how clean it might in fact be, metamorphoses, coming off the top of the head, into laundry. They are not surprised and it elicits no remark when that same laundry somehow transforms itself back into wearable clothes and appears again in their drawers, washed, dried, and folded.

Same with the dirty dishes that somehow end up clean again, day after day, and back in the cupboards. The food supplies, my family members appear to believe, replenish themselves of their own accord. The scattered newspapers, sandals, poker chips, and half-chewed dog bones that were right there on the living room floor just yesterday, oddly aren't there now.

Does anybody besides me recognize that these things happen? Does anybody besides me know how? Has anyone in my

15

family or yours ever been heard to say, "Hey, look, isn't that empty spot right where I left my candy wrapper just a few days ago?"

Even though both my husband and I have lots of things to do to keep our business of a household running, it just seems to be the nature of things that my chores are comprised mostly of the invisible overhead, the lowly maintenance, the taken-for-granted infrastructure. Meanwhile my husband is out there showing off the exciting new product line.

Man may work from sun to sun, but women's work is never done, goes the old proverb. And to that I would just like to add, Even if it did get done, who would notice?

This disparity is not really my husband's fault, I know that. To be honest, I don't really want to dig the hole and plant the tree because I know that my husband, with his greater weight, superior strength, and better shovel can do it so much faster. And I'll even admit that I don't want my husband to do the laundry, because I want my white shirts to be white, not pink.

So here I am. This modern, liberated woman, doing so many of the exact same chores that June Cleaver was doing, without looking nearly as pert or having any cute aprons. Women's work, in other words. The affairs of Mrs. Michael A. Ferro.

At the same time, when I get finished folding the laundry, I'm pursuing a demanding writing career in a competitive environ-ment. Men's work, in other words. The affairs of the woman once known as Muffy Mead. Therein lies the dilemma of so many modern wives. How can we live up to both sets of expectations? How do we get it all done?

We modern-day wives, frankly, have got to let some things go by the wayside. Even if it makes us feel like slacker wives. I know that there's simply no way I can have a good marriage, raise my kids, and also meet my professional goals and obliga-tions if I'm trying to achieve the ideals of the domestic goddess of the 1950s in my "spare time." I know it's probably easy to scoff at that—but I think the domestic goddess of the 1950s has made a whopping comeback in recent times, and it gives me the jitters.

If you don't believe me, then just take a gander at what's on the covers of most women's magazines next time you're at the checkout counter replenishing the bread.

Almost all the magazine titles that are published exclusively for women are about the following subjects: cooking, decorating, raising children, and looking good. Looking good, in our time, is more about exuding frank unabashed sexuality than pertness, but with that exception, every one of these subjects is easily inside June Cleaver territory.

But wait—don't get the jitters yet. Because what's most frightening about this state of affairs is that it wouldn't even be enough, by today's standards, to do any of these things—cooking, decorating, raising children, or looking good—at June Cleaver's level.

Let's face it, June Cleaver was no Martha Stewart. Mrs. Cleaver may have been able to whip up a delicious lemon pie, but were they tree-ripened Meyer Lemons? Were they freshly squeezed in a chrome and stainless steel commercial juicer? Did she layer her pastry with unsalted organic butter? Did she wield her own culinary blowtorch over the meringue to brown each perfect peak to the optimum shade of goldenness? I don't think so. June Cleaver probably just threw the whole pie in under the broiler and let it brown unevenly.

Now that I think about it, old June wasn't such a domestic goddess after all. She was more of a slacker.

It seems like when it comes to all of these "women's" endeavors such as cooking, entertaining, and decorating, we're now supposed to adhere to performance standards that could only be achieved by outright professionals. So I shouldn't make an example of Martha

Stewart, because making perfect pies from scratch, or more accurately, supervising a staff of people who make perfect pies from
scratch, actually *is* her profession. The only thing I never liked about
her is that she acts like I should do it too. The same way.

Since I work outside my home, I only have time to make
homemade lemon pies on very rare occasions. But at this point
my husband might ask when have I ever made a lemon pie, so let
me preempt him by acknowledging that I have, in fact, never
made one. But that's just because I happen to think store-bought
pies are surprisingly good.

All right, all right, Mr. Michael A. Ferro—it's also because I
don't know how to make pie. I'm just making the point that even
if I were so inclined, lemon meringue pie is too time-consuming to
fit into my schedule on a regular basis.

But let's not get bogged down in pie. I also don't have the
time, the required schooling, or the necessary equipment to throw
lavish thematic dinner parties, or make elaborate dried-flower
arrangements, or even whip up "simple" lavender sachets for all
our underwear drawers in the ways that are so beguilingly presented in women's magazines. I'm not even sure I could sew
rick-rack on towels. And I just wonder what busy woman would
even *try* to operate at that ambitious level on a regular basis.

Maybe it's just a cry for visibility. Maybe we wives are hoping that if we arrange the vegetables in a pyramid garnished with herb sprigs and looking like they were just flown in from the kitchen of Chez Panisse, our family members will actually sit up and take notice. Maybe that's why we watch the television shows that tell us how to do these things. Maybe we think it would even put us on par with the person who hangs light fixtures.

But I don't know, and I'll probably not find out, because I almost never have time to julienne the zucchini. And I don't believe that's just because I have a career. The stay-at-home moms I know can't perform at the *Better Homes & Garden* level, either. Not in all the ways we're supposed to. So it's easy for all of us modern-day wives to feel like slacker wives. We don't have it in us, or in our schedules, to be Mrs. Ward Cleavers, and in the meantime she's turned out to be an underperformer anyway.

At our house, that means I often won't have dinner on the table when my husband gets home from work. It means he might even get home from work before I do. And it means that I might even inquire of him, as I stroll through the door, "Do we have bread?"

Fortunately for me, my husband would never get irritated by my asking such a question. On top of that, he's inherently fair. He understands why our house isn't clean most of the time, and why I get behind on the laundry, and why it seems like we're always out of bread.

He realizes, in other words, that he's got himself a slacker wife. Someone who knows she can't be the domestic goddess of the 1950s—much less of the current day—at the same time she's working at an outside job. Someone who loves her husband and kids, but doesn't always manage to get a hot meal on the table for them. Someone who makes her marriage a priority (while asking the same of her husband), but who has a lot of other priorities as well.

What I'm trying to do at the end of the day is set my own priorities. And what I'm trying really hard to do is to set them without comparing myself to the model of domestic achievement presented by magazines and TV commercials.

All I can say is, Mr. Michael A. Ferro still seems to love me. So I must be doing something right.

chapter 2

Can we talk dirty?

—2—

I would like to just go ahead and start this chapter with my first confession. A real bombshell, probably: I didn't take a shower today.

Whether or not I showered yesterday is probably not even worth mentioning, since I know I've already crossed a line that might have me excluded from neighborhood dinner parties and maybe even my own book club. So I won't mention it.

But clean is a relative term, and by my own standards I'm clean. I'd like to elaborate more on my standards in a moment, but for now let me just say that I can live with the fact that I may not be clean by society's standards, because I think I have some idea, from twenty years in advertising, who's creating those standards.

It's not we consumers. It's not even people who might know better than we do about such things. Healthcare professionals, for instance. No, those who are creating the current standards of bodily cleanliness in our culture are the manufacturers and marketers of bodily cleaning products. None of us will ever be clean by their standards, because it would mean a precipitous drop in the sales of shampoos, tongue scrapers, wet wipes, deodorant soaps, cotton swabs, exfoliators, depilatories, and douche.

We can't have a drop in the sales of douche.

Or can we? People in other countries don't seem to be nearly as obsessive as Americans about continually cleaning themselves, every nook and cranny. People I've met in the most culturally refined cities of Europe think Americans are cuckoo in this regard, that we're dangerously close to becoming an entire nation of Howard Hugheses.

Perhaps it's just a matter of defining the word *clean*, and the word *dirty*, since they're both relative terms. Maybe every person has to define these terms for themselves. I know I have.

Here's a little mental exercise: Let's say you showered, but then you sweated over a pot of boiling pasta. Are you dirty now? What if you cooked the pasta, then lay down on the living room rug on your stomach to watch TV? Do you now need to take another shower? What if, after you perspired over the pasta and got up off the rug, you then walked around the block and a city bus drove by in close proximity? Are you dirty now, for sure?

I know a lot of people would say, "Yes, filthy dirty. You need to be washed, deodorized, and defumigated, and your clothes do too." I know that people shower over cleaner circumstances than I've just described, every day.

You're still clean enough by my standards, though. I don't think a little sweat, accompanied by a thin layer of household dust, even when added to by a microscopic application of diesel smog, makes you all that dirty.

But don't ask me, because according to my standards my own hair is clean. And as I said, I didn't even wash it today. I think it was the man who used to cut my hair that first gave me the idea I could opt out of what seems to be our national obsession with cleanliness. I was sitting down for a haircut and started complaining about the condition of my hair—always dry, always brittle—when he suggested, "Just stop washing it all the time."

Alarmed, I asked, "But what will happen?"

"Nothing," he answered. "It'll be healthier."

"You mean washing my hair is not good for it?!"

"No it's not," he continued, "and the oil from your scalp, if you would just brush it through vigorously, would be the best possible conditioner for your dry hair."

You talk about a bombshell. Once I started weaning myself from my daily shampooing, I found that he was right. My hair looked better and felt better. Not only that, his suggestion has, in the years since I implemented it, saved me a lot of time and money. What a relief it was to be let off the hook in that way. Cleansing, really.

I realize my great success with dirty hair has partly to do with the fact that my skin and hair have a tendency to be dry anyway, but it made me think. It made me think about why I had willy-nilly been doing what I assumed every other woman was doing without asking myself whether or not it really worked for me. It made me want to reexamine a lot of the other things in my grooming routine.

And that, as I've already admitted, has led me down the road to ruin. It's now to the point where I not only don't bathe every day, I also don't exfoliate every day and I don't even shave every day. Haven't douched in a decade. If the federal government got hold of me, I'd probably be named as a Superfund site.

But constant personal grooming is not the only cleanliness obsession I've chucked. Because it's not just our bodies (especially women's bodies) these days that are supposed to be spotless, hairless, odorless, and scraped entirely free of any dead or dying skin cells. Our houses and their entire contents, if we are to be good wives, must always be microscopically clean, according to television commercials and magazine ads. Never mind that this is, from a factual standpoint, impossible. It's still the goal.

You can confirm this for yourself by turning on your TV, especially if you turn it on between the hours of ten in the morning and three in the afternoon. We all know where the term *soap opera* comes from. It comes from the fact that daytime television programming has traditionally been paid for by the advertisers of cleaning products.

This programming for women has not been paid for by the advertisers of cars, sad to say, or the advertisers of sexy shoes, Mediterranean cruises, or laptop computers—all things that I personally, along with my other women friends, could get excited about buying.

No, we've gotten the soaps courtesy of soaps. Soaps, detergents, cleansers, solvents. Yes, I do buy these items, but is it exciting? It's not exciting. And I'm even less excited by the underlying message for the viewers, which is, "If you're home during the day, Mrs., the least you should be doing is the laundry and house cleaning."

I'll never forget a campaign, created by a famous ad man (although I probably don't need to mention that he was a man) for a cleaning product that addressed that age-old scourge of humanity, "ring-around-the-collar." Actually, that was never an age-old scourge of humanity; it was a problem that was mostly hatched by the ad itself so it could be solved by the product. The commercial depicted a husband and wife on vacation, but with all the fun spoiled when the tour guide pointed out, aghast, that the husband's shirt had ring-around-the-collar. At that point in the commercial, everyone, including the ill-mannered tour guide, the nosy passersby, and the camera itself, zeroed in on the guilty party.

If you were born too late to have seen this commercial, you might assume I'm referring to the husband with the sweaty neck when I say "guilty party." And if so, I really love you for it. But the guilty party, as we Baby Boomers remember, was the wife. The wife, whose responsibility it was to make certain that everyone's clothes were clean, even while they were being worn. The wife, so derelict in her duties that she had let such a socially disastrous thing as ring-around-the-collar befall her husband. The wife, with whom those women watching the commercial were actually supposed to identify, and lamentably they probably did.

Of course, in the next scene the bad wife redeemed herself by heavily dousing the offending collar with the prescribed application of blue chemicals, specifically formulated to eliminate this particular horror. Even the tour guide was satisfied with the results, which for some reason seemed to be important.

I wasn't married at the time this commercial was on the air, but I remember that it made me nervous and suspicious. Yikes, I thought, is this what I have to look forward to once I've got a husband? Do men not have any idea how to keep their own stuff clean? And in any case, wouldn't constant cleaning be an egregious waste of all my expensive education and professional experience? Is that what marriage is all about?

Now that I'm married, I know that keeping your husband's clothes fresh and clean is not what marriage is all about. Not for me, anyway. But whenever I'm home during the day and happen to turn on the TV, I still see the same kind of guilt-fueled messages as "ring-around-the-collar" from the soap opera advertisers. And it's a reminder that one thing I am supposed to do as a wife and mother is keep our house and its contents, including all of our clothes, clean.

Okay, fine. I'll give it a go. But conveniently for me, clean doesn't mean what it means to the advertisers. Conveniently for me, I think they're nuts. From watching television or reading magazines, one would get the idea that every identifiable item in the house, whether solid, liquid, or gas, needs to be utterly clean. The carpet fibers ("deep down"), the sofa upholstery, the air, the toilet bowl, the baseboards, the inside of the oven, the tile grout . . . all of these need to be clean, and fortunately there's a chemical solution formulated for every last item.

I know that sometimes cleaning can be rewarding and even cathartic. Sometimes it actually feels good, and maybe that's a good reason to do it. But it seems to me that the American woman is being driven by chemical manufacturers to accept a cleanliness standard that's not only unnecessary, but that truly has a downside in terms of time, money, and cost to the environment.

No matter what the item, and no matter if you're doing the job yourself or have a housekeeping service, the standards have gotten ridiculously—perhaps dangerously—high. Because when the advertisers say "clean," they mean without so much as a smudge, a germ, or a speck of dust. Clean, as though no dirty human being with their grubby hands has ever used or even touched them. Like new!

Why is it that cleanliness so often seems to translate to, "like new"? "Like new" is a phrase that's often used to convince us of the effectiveness of a cleaning product. I guess the assumption is that things are at their best when they're new. That a cooking pot, for instance, is utterly best before it has ever been on a fire or had icky food in it.

I don't know why that should be so. I've noticed that many things tend to age pretty well, and sometimes get quite a bit better as I use them. My own mother's frying pans were cast iron, and I never even saw them when they were shiny and new. They weren't expensive, but they were indestructible.

I happen to have two of them in my own cupboard right now. They must be nearly fifty years old, and they've only gotten blacker and better with age. By the time they were handed down to me, they had become so well-seasoned—some would say dirty—that a frying egg wouldn't even stick to them. Take that, Teflon. I wouldn't dream of trying to get them completely clean, and I definitely don't want them to be like new.

So I don't think it's a given that everything has to be completely clean, because some things are actually better dirty. My hair, my frying pans. But even if I did manage to get every item clean and keep it that way, I'd only be halfway there according to the marketers of chemicals. Because the items in our household must not only be clean, they also need to smell pretty. Or "fresh," as the marketing vernacular goes. I believe the concept of fresh actually trumps the concept of clean, because we now have quite a few products—aerosol sprays, plug-in devices, laundry additives, and fabric sprays—that don't really have anything to do with making things clean. They just make things fresh. So whether or not something is the least bit clean, it can be fresh.

This is fantastic because now anything—even a box of cat feces—can be fresh. Must be fresh! Our cats expect it, I've seen that on TV. I know how huffy they can get when the smell of their poop is not masked. Needless to say I don't have any problem with people who want to mask the smell of cat poop. Please go ahead, in fact, by all means. But if cat poop can be fresh then, honestly, what is fresh?

Judging from the package descriptions in the cleaning aisle at the grocery store, one would gather that fresh means it smells like "Spring Rain." But did the product development people who came up with the scent of Spring Rain ever go outside and smell rain in the spring or any other time of year? Did they take any notes on what a garden, or a driveway, or a bird's nest, or the suburbs smell like when they're wetted down?

I guess fresh is not meant to be the actual scent that's promised. I guess fresh must really mean smelling like a bunch of chemicals. That shouldn't surprise us, though, because a bunch of chemicals is about all we're getting when we buy products that make things fresh.

Personally, I don't feel it's necessary for all things to be clean or fresh. Maybe that's because I grew up on a cattle ranch, where the presence of cow manure or the smell of a horse stall was not considered distasteful. Nobody said, "Eew, where's the Lysol?" when they walked into the barn. We didn't have cow manure in our house as I recall, not for extended periods anyway, but life on a ranch gave me some perspective that's come in very handy, and it's that good smells and bad smells are relative and subjective. And the same goes for what's supposedly clean, and what's supposedly dirty.

Once you've decided that cow manure is not necessarily dirty, you can see how that would set the bar pretty low for cleanliness in general.

I know in the case of my own mom that she had too much to do between herding cows, stacking hay, and getting food on the table to even begin to live up to the current standards of cleanliness, whether for her person, her house, or our clothes. I doubt that most wives of a generation ago, ranchers or not, stay-at-home or not, were held to nearly the same standards of cleanliness as wives today. But all I can personally testify to is how it was at our house.

At our house, if you wore your jeans to school one day, that didn't by definition mean they were dirty. If you wore them while branding calves, then yes, they got washed. In hot water and a batch of chemicals, with no apologies. It was the only way to remove the smell of burned hair and the mixed stains of vaccine, manure, mud, and blood.

I've read that specific memories can often be triggered by odors. The odor of branding is one that's imprinted on my memory cells to stay. I know that to most people, there are probably few smells more distasteful than burned hair. But I'm here to tell you, you can get used to it. I'm not claiming it smells good, any more than cow manure does, but after a while it doesn't smell so bad either.

Maybe that's because of the positive associations it has for me. The singular smell of burned hair brings back memories of branding with the rest of my family, working together year after year in that rite of spring. Yes, to me, the smell of branding is the smell of spring. Maybe that's why I don't agree with the chemical manufacturers on what spring is supposed to smell like. Don't worry, I do realize most people would come down on their side and not mine in this matter, but it's still a subjective call.

We almost always branded on Saturdays or Sundays in order that my brothers and I would not have to miss school, because our contribution was actually important. So we worked side by side: my dad, my mom, my two brothers, and me. And also side by side with ranch hands who were often like extended family. These are wonderful memories for me, and that includes all the noises, dirt, and smells. We could brand nearly a hundred calves an hour in an orchestrated effort that only worked if everyone involved knew exactly where they were supposed to be, and when. Keeping up that kind of pace is pretty remarkable when you consider that branding meant branding, dehorning, vaccinating, ear-tagging, castrating, and dewlapping.

If you're not a cowgirl, I should explain that dewlapping is cutting a thin flap of skin from a calf's throat, so that it hangs down like the dewlap, or wattle, that a moose comes by naturally. We used to summer our cows on a vast, fenceless range where they could mingle with cattle from several other ranches. When it came time in the fall to round them up and sort them out, it helped us that our cattle had dewlaps, because it's a differentiating mark that, unlike a brand, can be seen from far away, and from either side.

I'm not even a cowgirl myself anymore. And I rarely get the opportunity to help my brothers brand calves. But my memories of branding are so positive that from my perspective it's a good smell, and if the smell of burned hair isn't categorically bad, I don't know what is. I'm not trying to sell you on it, though. I'm just worried that we've gotten to the point in our culture where almost anything other than man-made perfume smells bad to us. Cooked broccoli, wet dogs, fresh fish, human beings—all these things just stink up the place.

Of course, they can all be freshened right up with a quick spray of chemicals. But not by me. I don't really want my kids, when they get to be adults, to have every memory triggered by the scent of Febreze. So I don't buy the plug-in air fresheners or the fabric sprays. And I really can't stand the perfumed pieces of cardboard you're supposed to hang from the rearview mirror of your car. This is a subjective statement, but I think all of those smell categorically bad.

It's not that I think it's okay to smell offensive to other people. Like I said, my mother didn't send us to school in the same clothes we branded in without washing them first. But my mom sure didn't use her washer and dryer as often as modern wives do. In fact, I remember she hated to use the latter. We had a clothesline in our back yard, and that was the clothes-drying method she preferred.

This embarrassed me, I'm ashamed now to say. You could see the clothesline and our laundry from the dirt road that curved up through our ranch. Bed sheets, T-shirts, underclothes, and dish-towels flapping in the breeze. I was sure that every kid on the school bus, as it stopped in the afternoon to let us off at the end of our driveway, was inspecting our family's clothes, mentally matching them up to their wearers, including me. Thank goodness my mother had some misgivings about brassieres dangling from the line. It didn't stop her from hanging them, but she folded them first so they didn't broadcast their shape quite as clearly.

But I remember tying the clothespin bag around my waist and going out with her to bring in the clean, dry laundry. I remember how the fabrics had a wonderful stiffness and smelled good—yes, fresh, if you know what I mean—and I always found myself burying my face in the basket for one heady, deep breath as I car-ried the laundry in to be folded.

I wish I weren't too vain to put a clothesline in our suburban back yard, but I admit I'm afraid of what the neighbors might think about T-shirts on the line, never mind bras.

My grandmother didn't worry about stuff like that. Her neighbors were miles away, but in any case she didn't have a dryer. My grandmother not only did not have a dryer, she didn't even have a washing machine when she married my grandfather in 1934 and moved with him into the bunkhouse. She was raised in Sheridan, Wyoming, which by Wyoming standards was a progressive, sizable city, and it was a leap of faith for this city girl to move to a cattle ranch five miles outside of Jackson Hole, a town of fewer than 1,000 people. The winters were long and when there was snow on the road, the trip to town could not be undertaken without a list of good reasons, because you made the trip sitting in a saddle or aboard a sleigh drawn by a strong but slow team of horses. So my grandmother didn't go to town more than a couple of times during the long winter.

When she did go, it's safe to say she didn't buy any detergents formulated just for ring-around-the-collar. She actually made her own laundry soap, according to the method she learned from her pioneer-stock mother-in-law, Sylvia. They saved all the animal fat from the household for making this soap. In that regard, being on a cattle ranch provided an advantage. She melted the fat to liquid in a big vat over a wood fire, and then combined the rendered fat with lye to make a solid, which was then formed and cut into bars for soap.

I asked my grandmother one time if she used the lye soap for household cleaning jobs as well as for laundry. Say, for mopping the floor.

"I didn't bother with mopping the floor," she replied.

"What do you mean?" I asked. "You mean you didn't do it every day?"

"No," she said, "I never did it."

Well. I guess that makes me look pretty good, even though I didn't take a shower today. But my grandmother is, if anything, more elegant and refined than most women I know, certainly more elegant and refined than I am. She simply happens to be pragmatic. And thinking about her always helps me regain my perspective on how much cleaning is really necessary. When she and my grandfather were living in the bunkhouse, she had her priorities, and a futile attempt to keep the bunkhouse floor mopped when ranch hands and family members were continually tromping in from the corral wasn't one of them. A quick sweep with a straw broom every once in a while was all you needed to get the big pieces out the door, and that was about the best you could expect.

In the six years my grandmother lived in the bunkhouse, she had two babies, a boy and a girl, and somehow they did just fine even though their mother never scrubbed the floor. I know that seems so utterly fantastic that some people would actually find it hard to believe.

"A baby can survive if the mom doesn't mop the floor?! Next you'll be saying babies don't need to have their binkies boiled every time they drop them on the dirty floor!" Yes, I probably will, but not until chapter seven.

Don't get me wrong. I mop my own floors from time to time, and my grandmother, when she finally moved out of the bunkhouse and into a home of her own with a linoleum floor, did too. But I tell her story just to make the comparison. Our gener-ation of women, or more accurately our generation of chemical marketers, is setting the standards of cleanliness impossibly high. But thinking back to my grandmother's and even my mother's day has made me realize that life for our family will continue without any dire consequences if my floor is not as clean as I imagine everyone else's is.

My grandmother did keep the clothes clean, according to the standards at the time, for her husband and children. But in her day, clothes didn't need to be washed until they'd been worn sev-eral times. The only laundry items that got washed after just one wearing were diapers. These she washed by hand in a tin tub, scrubbing up and down against a washboard in a harsh solution of hot water and her lye soap.

That sounds plenty tedious, but washing the diapers was a lark compared to drying them. In the winter, drying diapers was a three-phase process. First, you wrung. You twisted until your muscles gave out, then twisted back the other way. Every bit of water that wasn't forced from the cloth would turn to ice on the clothesline. And no matter how well you'd wrung, the diapers came in from the clothesline as stiff as boards. Then my grandmother would hang them up on a second line, an inside line strung in her living room behind the wood stove. Finally, they'd be dry and pliable enough for folding. And shortly, dirtying.

A few years into her marriage, my grandmother actually did get a washing machine, and it had a wringer too. My grandmother's father was never able to leave Sheridan and visit her on the ranch, and who knows how he really envisioned her situation at that primitive outpost. But from the time of her marriage she wrote faithfully to her father and mother back in her hometown, describing her life on the ranch and what everyone was doing.

In one letter, she mentioned that her husband was across the yard at his parents' house, listening to a radio program. A few weeks later, here came a radio from the Sears catalog, courtesy of her father.

In another letter, my grandmother closed by saying, "Well, I'd better get over to Sylvia's to finish up my laundry, so I'll write again later."

Pretty soon, a Sears washing machine was delivered to the ranch for my grandmother, to her surprise, delight, and chagrin. Even today, as my grandmother tells this story, she feels sheepish because she hadn't intended to drop hints about such things as her lack of a washing machine. And after the radio and washing machine incidents, she was very careful about describing her circumstances on the ranch without making it sound like she needed something.

Because she didn't really feel needy. She had only to think about the way her mother-in-law had had to do things when her seven children were small to feel lucky. To my grandmother, life was relatively easy and the chores were doable, even though it took seven days of her week to complete them.

Of course, I have a washing machine, and a dryer, and an electric iron, and even a hand-held steamer to get wrinkles out of sweaters. So if I compare my laundry situation to my grandmother's, I know I should feel a lot luckier than she felt. And I do feel lucky, with one important exception. That is that in my grandmother's day, people actually wore their clothes more than one time. I can imagine how this provided their owners with an incentive to take care of them and keep them somewhat clean, an incentive which no one in my family seems to have.

Doing laundry by hand on the ranch in the 1930s as my grandmother describes it was an awful lot of trouble compared to how I do it today. But does the fact that it's now mostly automated justify continually doing it? If you ask me, it still takes up way too much time. Technology might have made it easier to do a load of laundry, but unfortunately the demand for ever cleaner clothes has outpaced the technological strides to the point where, ironically, the women I know actually spend more time doing washing than my grandmother did.

I guess they think they have to keep up. Personally, I've gotten in the habit of turning clothes in the laundry basket back to their owners if they don't meet my standards of dirtiness. What an epiphany—wearing your clothes more than one time!

It means Joe and Belle often appear at school a bit wrinkled, but so what? I'm sure there will come a time when they'll care more about their clothes and appearance than I do, and considering my waning interest, it'll probably come sooner for them than for other kids.

Joe and Belle, at the ages of four and five years old, respectively, helped with branding last spring for the first time. The calves were bigger than I remembered them being when I was little. Their rumps were at the same height as Joe's shoulder, and I had some mixed feelings about letting him down in the holding pen with them. But he was determined to help with what his older cousin and the other boys were doing, wrestling the calves into the chutes so they could be lined up to get branded.

After a few hours of that he was tarred with manure front and back. His sweaty face had been coated with fine brown corral dirt. The thick smell of singed cowhide had permeated his jacket, pants, and hair. His teeth and the insides of his nostrils were lined with black. Michael, Belle, and I were just as bad. It set a new standard for the three of them on just how dirty and stinky a person could get, especially when they were having such a good time.

This has been quite useful to me.

Now when Michael thinks his jeans are dirty, I can say, "Dirty? That's not dirty, come back tomorrow." Now when the babysitter asks if the kids need to have baths, I can say, "No thanks, I think they're still pretty clean." Now if someone mentions the lingering odor of last night's baked salmon, I can say, "The world smells. Isn't that wonderful? Breathe deep!"

chapter 3

Old enough to know better

-3-

I'm sure that, like me, you've heard about the alarming loss of
self-esteem that often occurs among teen girls who are constantly bombarded with media images of impossibly beautiful and
absurdly thin young women. These images have the potential to
create both mental and physical health problems for young girls,
the reports say, because for the vast majority of them, there's no
amount of dieting, exercise, or thigh cream that would ever
enable them to look like the female bodies they see in magazines
and on TV.

The problem, they say, is that for almost all teenage girls, the
portrayals of womanhood presented by the mass media are just
completely unrealistic.

Excuse me, but for teenage girls? The supermodel standards
are unrealistic for teenage girls? Are they just completely down
to earth, then, for those of us who are over thirty? I dare say that
if the cover of *Cosmo* makes the average teenage girl feel inadequate, then it should be no surprise if it makes forty-four-year-old

women like myself want to hang ourselves from the rafters with a thong.

Not that I would ever do such a thing, but I must congratulate myself on having come up with a functional purpose for a thong.

The truth is, now that I'm in my mid-forties I've discovered I don't have complete control over my body, despite what *Shape* magazine says, and I certainly have less control than I did in my teens. I don't just mean the startling bouts of incontinence that followed childbearing I mean I literally woke up one day to find a jiggly spare tire down around my middle, with extra padding on both sides of my lower back. And I swear I've done absolutely nothing to bring this upon myself. In fact, I actually still do sit-ups. I've never eaten a box of Krispy Kremes. I've never been a couch potato. I simply arrived at my mid-forties, exactly on schedule. And my body at this point started acquiring peculiar characteristics, completely of its own accord, and quite suddenly I might add.

Obviously, what's happening to me must be the result of a very powerful force in the universe. So naturally I'm skeptical of the media messages that tell me I'm supposed to try and fight it. But they sure tell me to. I hardly ever see any women who look like they're even in my age group on the covers of magazines, or on TV shows, or in clothing catalogs. I have to look at all the same beautiful young models in the media that teenage girls are looking at. I see the ads for serums that reduce the "appearance" of wrinkles, and I've noticed that they don't ever feature women that actually have wrinkles. Honestly, most of them look like teenagers to me.

I know, I know. That's supposed to make me think the serums truly do what's promised. Of course they're not going to show women my age what we *really* look like, even though I'm right in the sweet spot of their target audience. I'm sure their marketing handbook says to show me what I will certainly *never* look like, but what I must surely *aspire* to look like. I know from my own years in marketing that this might mean more time is spent digitally enhancing the photograph than taking the photograph, but it's time well-spent for the advertisers. Just printing what's on the raw film would be a waste of their money. If they showed us what forty-year-old skin really looks like, serums or not, we wouldn't buy their products, because we'd quickly deduce that they were a waste of *our* money.

But I don't think the digital enhancement of photographs is the most insidious thing about ads for beauty products anyway. I think the most insidious thing about advertising campaigns for so many beauty products is that they put the unscientific idea into your head that unfortunate occurrences such as wrinkled skin are actually a choice. That aging itself is—at least for us women—optional. You can have power over this process, the products promise us, so let us help you take control.

Otherwise what are you going to do, just surrender? Throw in the towel? Sit there and look your real age and basically be a complete slacker of a woman? No, you must "fight it every step of the way," to quote a face cream commercial. I'm sure that's why women my age are buying so much more thigh cream than the teenagers, and why we're spending a lot more on plastic surgery, Botox, and chemical peels than they are. We're older, but we can't accept it. We've bought into the idea that aging according to the inevitable passing of time is something we can, and should, simply choose not to do.

But whom would we be making that choice for? Ourselves? Other women? Our husbands? That darling young hard body we buy a latté from three mornings a week? Maybe fingers should be pointed at all of the above, starting with ourselves, but let's talk about husbands for a moment since we're on the subject of wives. It used to be that a wife was supposed to look good for her husband, if she wanted to keep a tight grip on him, and I'm afraid that idea hasn't gone completely out of fashion.

I remember hearing the news about the breakup of an acquaintance's marriage several years ago. I felt like groaning, or maybe more like kicking the person I was talking to sharply in the kneecap, when they excused the fact that the husband had decided to leave his wife of fourteen years with this cryptic explanation: She let herself go.

Let herself go. Mmm-*hmm*. This euphemistic phrase, apparently, didn't need to be clarified. She let herself go. Although I guess we can assume, if we're feeling kind, that this woman probably didn't want to go and didn't intend to go. But when she started to go, she didn't stop herself and that was her crime. She did the unthinkable by permitting herself to go, and thus, inevitably, she went.

But where did she go? That's the question I wanted to hear the answer to. Did she simply go forward in time? Did she— eeek—age? Did she do what most human beings do as they get older, gaining a few pounds, getting a bit wrinkled, and graying around the temples? What an appalling lack of discipline she must have had. Apparently she did not heed any of the advertising messages from beauty products manufacturers who are telling us that aging is a condition we can avoid if we will just hand over our wallets.

I don't really think aging is an option, however. Not for women, and not for men. In fact, if where this wife went was simply forward in time, should we not assume that her husband, over the course of fourteen years, went with her? Or was her husband miraculously exempt from the ticking of his (and how I wish everyone would acknowledge that men have one too) biological clock? I suspect he wasn't. What he was probably exempt from was the obligation to "fight it every step of the way."

The husband in this story, as in so many stories, was not held to the same aesthetic standards as the wife, and frankly it only took one look at him to determine that. The wife might have been there to look young and lovely, but not the husband. He must have been bringing something else to the table. The bacon, I assume.

The wife was the one cooking the bacon, naturally, and she was serving it to the family members, and she was cleaning up after them when they had finished. But those kinds of contributions weren't enough, in the end, because as she did all these things for her family, she wasn't looking sufficiently like the girl her husband married fourteen years earlier, and I guess he felt wronged. So she lost her husband. And, too bad for him, he lost her. I don't know if he was better off, but I always assumed that she was.

The same probably can't be said for the television news anchor in our market who also let herself go by succumbing to the passage of time and lost her job. She's probably not better off. She was just one of many female news anchors who've come and gone at that particular news desk over the past twenty years. Just one in a long string to sit for a relatively short time beside her former colleague, the male coanchor.

This is an amazing man whose own career shows no signs of slowing. The issue of aging is not an issue for him. He just keeps going strong after more than forty years—yes, forty years, practically since the invention of television itself—on the job. I'm not saying he doesn't have crow's feet and gray hair, because he has them both in abundance. But so what? He's not there to look like a twenty-year-old, he's there to give us the news, and what we television viewers want from a reporter is credibility. Does he know what he's talking about? That's what we're concerned with. We're watching the program to get reliable information, not to be titillated by youth and beauty, so we demand the utmost in credibility. You throw in good diction and grammar, and you've got yourself a reporter! Or at least you do if that reporter is a man.

This man's new female coanchor, the one who replaced the woman who must have erroneously thought it would be okay to develop her own crow's feet, is nearly thirty years younger than he is and wasn't even born when he got his first job in journalism. Yet for some reason the decision-makers at the television station decided this was a pairing that made sense. Her youthful beauty cancels out her lack of experience, while his experience makes up for his more advanced age. This is fair because women and men, in what must be the station manager's view, should bring two different things to the table.

It might be my own personal quirk, but I don't think that's any way to run a railroad. The wife, and the female news anchor, were probably both just hitting their strides. Just when the wife of fourteen years had done most of the hard work raising the children and could finally find more time for herself and for her relationship with her husband, she was replaced. Just when the news anchor had logged enough time in front of the camera to have earned the same credibility as her male coanchor, she got booted. If this is the way things work, then not only are we women getting shortchanged, but so is everyone around us.

Too often it is the way things work, or perhaps I should say the way things fall stupidly apart. For all we've done to achieve equality in recent decades, women still have far more to lose than men, in our relationships and in our careers, by gaining weight, by not being beautiful, or by simply aging according the natural pas-sage of the years. Beauty, at a time when youth equals beauty, is still one of the most important things we're supposed to bring to the table.

But alas, we can't deliver, because at least in one respect we're all *letting ourselves go*. We're letting ourselves go the exact same place where the jilted wife let herself go. Forward in time. We can't help it, actually, nighttime-repair creams notwithstanding.

One bit of recompense is that our husbands can't help it either. Personally, I would never have married someone who wanted me just for my ornamental qualities. I'm completely con-fident that my husband Michael married me for my colossal and alluring mind. When we're alone together, there's nothing he'd rather do than exchange ideas on issues of deep intellectual sig-nificance late into the night. Isn't that right, dear?

But just in case my husband ever veers into more superficial territory, now that I'm in my mid-forties, I've taken to carrying a hand-mirror with me at all times. No, no—not so I can regularly

assess my own appearance—but so that if my husband ever suggests I'm not the gal I used to be, I won't have to go to the
trouble of making superfluous remarks because I can just hand
him the mirror.

But I don't think that'll be necessary, because my husband
says he likes the way I look, even though at forty-four I look
every bit my age. I don't have quite as many wrinkles as my mother did at forty-four, but that's because I have a desk job, and she
worked outside all her life. She had all the character, beauty, and
individuality of someone who'd spent dry Wyoming winters and
high-altitude summers in the agrarian outdoors. She died on
horseback the day she turned sixty-one, so I will never get to see
how she would have aged into her seventies and eighties. But at
sixty, I thought she was very pretty. I would love to look the way
she did, and thanks to a genetic predisposition over which I have
no control, I probably will age about the same way.

The day after my mother died, my brothers and I gathered
ourselves and spent the afternoon at her house, choosing which
photos would be on display at her memorial service, which would
be given to our small-town newspaper, which would appear in
the program at the church. The outcome of this melancholy exercise provided a broader perspective, for me, on beauty.

My mother had led a prolific life, growing up on her parents' cattle ranch and then running her own ranch for more than thirty years. On the ranch as well as off, she was not afraid of much and she was interested in everything. She was one of the first people I knew or heard of to buy a personal computer. She was one of the first people I knew to bungee-jump. She ran for elective office several times, and although she never won any statewide office, she never let defeat stop her from running again.

So we had a wide variety of photos to sort through, from the numerous and varied adventures of her life, and it was not easy to decide which handful of them would best represent the versatile woman she was.

There was even an 8" x 10" glossy that had been on a magazine cover. During her early thirties, my mother's picture had been taken for the cover of *Farm Journal* magazine. *Farm Journal* is obviously not *Cosmopolitan*, or even *Good Housekeeping*, but she had a brilliant smile, and I decided that was my favorite picture of her. She looked so all-American beautiful in this portrait of her, in a natural, outdoorsy kind of way.

But my younger brother Matt picked out a different picture. It was no professional portrait, just a snapshot. It showed my mother in her middle fifties, perhaps not cover girl material any more, not even for *Farm Journal*. She was riding in the back of somebody's pickup truck, and you could tell she was bouncing up and down because the picture was a little blurry and her hair was flying in every direction. Her face, for some reason, was spattered with black mud—even her teeth—but she was laughing like a hyena.

"This is my favorite picture of her," Matt said.

I looked at that picture of my mother with mud on her face and in her mouth and had to agree that in a way, his picture showed my unique mom at her most beautiful. It depicted pretty accurately the mom we would miss, the unaffected woman who was always so game and often so funny and always just herself. She had aged gracefully by then.

What I mean by that is that she had aged without pretending or wishing it was not happening. She wasn't always so concerned with her appearance, at least not as much as most women are. Not as much as I usually am, anyway. With her it was more about what she was doing, not how she looked while she did it. Maybe that's why she had so much fun and got so much accomplished.

That makes me want to look the way my mother did in the picture that Matt picked out. I want to look like my mother did in spite of the fact that none of the women on magazine covers look like she did.

I'm not complaining that you just never see them with black mud on their faces and teeth. It's more that they hardly ever look over twenty years old. And some of the celebrities on magazine covers are actually forty, fifty, or even (gasp) sixty. They just don't *look* it. Somehow, they've overcome the effects of aging. I don't mean to make this sound mysterious, because we all know that the most effective way to avoid looking your age is with plastic surgery, and if you're the type who tends to be featured on magazine covers and *are* over twenty years old, it's practically standard operating procedure, no pun intended.

Now that I've brought up the subject of plastic surgery, you might expect that I'm going to give it a good drubbing, along with all the women who've resorted to it, but I'm not. Because I don't think it's a bad thing for someone who's always hated her big bumpy nose to have it smoothed out. I don't think it's a bad thing for someone who's developed a giant drooping double chin to want to have it tucked in. I can see how it would relieve them of a certain burden.

The other reason I can't slam plastic surgery, though, is that I've had plastic surgery. I know from personal experience how a woman can justify risking her very life on the operating table for an elective procedure, as daft as that sounds. I went in for it because I decided it was the only way to make my butt look smaller. I don't even know that I can totally blame women's magazines for this, but I've believed ever since I was a teenager that I had an oversized behind.

When I went to address this defect twenty years later, however, I didn't go the direct route and get my butt liposuctioned. Rather, I got my breasts enlarged, on the grounds that it would balance things out. A brilliant strategy, really; kind of like sticking yourself with a pin so you won't feel so miserable about having the flu.

About three years later, after two pregnancies and after breast-feeding two babies, I'd developed enough scar tissue around my implants to make them feel like a pair of oranges in a pair of socks. If you've never experienced this, let me tell you that it gets old having two round balls attached to your front all the time. They kind of move out of the way when you lie down to sleep on your stomach, and they kind of don't. They don't look or feel much like breasts; they look and feel more like you have two bulbous foreign objects planted under your skin, which maybe shouldn't have surprised me. So anyway, I went to plastic surgeon number two and told him I wanted them taken out.

"I feel like I've got a pair of oranges in a pair of socks," I declared, having assumed an awkward sitting position on the exam table. "And I want them removed."

Not pulling any punches himself, sitting comfortably in his chair, he replied, "So your plan is to leave here with just the pair of socks, then."

And he proceeded to explain to me that, between the compression that had been caused by the implants themselves and the shrinkage of breast tissue that almost all women experience with breast-feeding, that would essentially be what I'd still have if I got the implants removed and left it at that. A pair of socks.

I produced a visual of that in my mind, contemplating my options for five or six seconds. I knew I wasn't dealing with knee-highs, definitely not. More like the flimsy little footies one wears while trying on shoes, the ones that barely come up to your bunions. But it wasn't the size of the socks that troubled me, it was the tendency of socks to be flat. So then, instead of having the implants removed, I had them replaced as per the plastic surgeon's recommendation.

They're smaller than the first go around and I'm happier with them. But I can report that none of this expensive and, to some extent, risky surgery has changed the size of my butt. I should also add that it took quite a while for my bank account to recover from this financial boondoggle. Breast augmentation starts at about three grand, and there are no free refills. The second pair costs just as much as the first.

The truth is, I wish I'd never had the plastic surgery in the first place. It did seem like a good idea at the time, both to me and to a girlfriend of mine who went under the knife for the same operation about a month after I did. But my friend feels the same way I do now, eight years later. What were we thinking? we've both asked ourselves. Why did we think bigger breasts would look better? They just look bigger. That's all. It's not like the breasts either of us were born with were a burden, a deformity. It wasn't the same as having a big bumpy nose or a giant double chin.

No one would ever go into a doctor's office and say, "I want bigger elbows; mine don't poke out enough." No one would ever say, "I want my knees enlarged, because I think it'll make my feet look smaller." Yet that's how absurd the idea of artificially enlarged breasts began to seem to me once I'd had them for a while.

I'm not pretending I don't know the significance of breasts. Of course breasts are different from elbows and knees, because

they're strictly female equipment, and they're the type of equipment that the men in our lives tend to fixate on. But I can't
blame my husband for my decision to get breast implants. We
weren't married at the time, but we were engaged. So I'd already
"snagged" him. And it wasn't his idea, it was mine. In fact I
remember clearly that when I was contemplating the surgery, he
expressed no opinion one way or the other, because he is no
dimwit.

So I didn't get breast augmentation to make me more attractive to my soon-to-be husband. I've already explained that my
main motivation was to shrink my butt in a roundabout kind of
way. But I wasn't doing *that* for the man I was about to marry
either. He says he likes my butt just fine. I've already said, he is
no dimwit. I was doing it not for him but for myself, because just
like so many women I know, I've *always* thought my butt was too
big. Why do so many of us women think our butts are too big?
Why do we ask our husbands that most treacherous question—
Do these make my butt look big?—whenever we put on a new
pair of pants?

My theory is that it's because fashion models have no
butts, and fashion models are the women we think we're supposed to look like. Of course we do; otherwise why are they

called models? Fashion models represent the ideal, the standard, the model after which we're supposed to pattern ourselves. They show us how clothes are meant to look, how the female body ought to be proportioned. If it were the standard to have butts, flabby arms, wrinkly faces, and gray hair, then we would see those things on the cover of *In Style,* wouldn't we? But we don't see them on the cover of *In Style,* because they're not in style.

At least they're not in style for women. Men are seldom photographed in gauzy gowns that are backless and strapless. But I did see Monica Lewinsky on the cover of a tabloid at the grocery store recently, entering a party in a backless, gauzy gown. I think the headline which ran margin-to-margin was "Monica Balloons!" And yes, from the three-quarters angle of her backside, it looked liked she'd gained some weight in the past year. I wouldn't be surprised if life had been a little stressful. But I'd like to see Bill Clinton in the same dress, photographed from the same angle. I'd like to see how his hairy, fat back and butt look in a halter dress, and it's too bad for Monica and the rest of us women that we never will. There's a double standard and there always has been. Maybe that's why men, somehow, seem better able to get away not only with fat backs but with aging too.

Our society seems to feel that men are more likely to still be attractive as they get older. I know that's a well-worn cliché, but I wouldn't dismiss it just because people keep repeating it. It's true. This must be why it's easier for men to get parts in movies or to keep their jobs as television reporters. This is what really bothers me. It makes no sense to me—not even from a biological, survival-of-the-species standpoint—for us wives to be held to a different standard of looking good than our husbands, particularly as we get older.

And what happens to women as we age, in an age when aging for women is so very out of style? These two things, at least: self-flagellation and spending. First we look at ourselves in the mirror and tell ourselves how horrible we look—how fat, how old, how completely unattractive. We beat ourselves up over it and often get literally depressed. And then we spend millions on exercise equipment and gym memberships, millions on night cream and acid wash, billions on elective plastic surgery in an effort to improve ourselves. And sometimes we improve ourselves to the point where we unwittingly turn ourselves into freaks of nature—but we're not slackers, by God, and we're going to keep hold of our men and our jobs.

I've fallen victim to this mentality myself, I've admitted that. Not only have I had plastic surgery, but I've been on a dozen diets. For me, there's nothing like going on a diet to bring on the most desperate feelings of starvation. I don't have to actually deprive myself of anything; it's the idea that I'm planning to deprive myself that makes me feel I'm in mortal peril.

"I'm going to croak if you don't eat a whole bag of Oreos right now" is the signal my body sends to my mind the minute I've made a decision to go on a low-carb diet. Oh my God, I think, I've got to obey this urge and save myself, because I can go on a diet tomorrow after this potentially fatal threat has passed.

You can see why weight-loss diets wouldn't tend to work for me. But from what I've read, they don't work for most people in the long term. And one thing they never do is stop the daily revolutions of our planet.

It's taken me a while, but I've finally realized that I started off life with a genetic program that's pretty much determined my basic shape and physical attributes and how I'm going to age. Exercise makes a difference, and so does eating well, but I'm still by and large turning into my mother.

So I try not to get depressed about the fact that I'm not ever going to look twenty years old again. I might as well get upset about never again looking like a three-year-old.

I'm not saying I no longer care about looking my best. I do. And certainly I want to be in good health. I just try to make sure

I keep in mind that "looking good" and "looking young" are two totally different things. No one would ever say about a nine-year-old, "She looks good for her age." Besides, more important than looking young, or looking good, is feeling good.

So I'm letting myself go, and getting another day older with every day that goes by—it never varies, not even by one day. I hope that doesn't make me a disappointment to my husband, in light of the fact that he's doing the exact same thing.

chapter 4

———◆———

Are we having fun yet?

-4-

About a year ago I was the assigned hostess for a committee meeting of about twenty other women, and I found myself, a few hours before they were to arrive for drinks and hors d'oeuvres, making a serious attempt to sponge the dirt from the word "ON" at the top of an old toggle light switch in our powder room. This was a feat I had to perform in near-darkness, for obvious reasons.

But what I remember with utter clarity is the following: It was very difficult to get the inside of the letter "O" clean. I'm sure at least some of the grime was seventy years old, and it was stuck inside that infernal little circle like black glue.

I finally ended up with a wire brush dipped in ammonia and that actually did the trick, but in my moment of triumph it occurred to me that I stood some chance of being electrocuted while performing this lunatic bit of cleaning I'd somehow worked myself into. I swear that all I'd set out to do, some twenty minutes before, was to spiff up the bathroom so I could have some people over and not leave the impression that my house was unkempt.

I slapped myself, figuratively of course, and sat down on the potty, exhausted. The amount of work I'd gone to just to make things nice for these women—friends, most of them, and non-judgmental, all of them—was laughable. At least I realized that much, at that moment. I also realized that I was so totally drained that what I really wanted to do was to go upstairs and lie back on my bed with a nice cup of tea and watch an episode of *Law & Order*, not socialize with twenty other women.

Not for the first time, I was too tired and too stressed out to have a good time at my own get-together. I'd not only cleaned the house top-to-bottom, including the rooms in which these women were certainly not going to set foot, but I'd also prepared way too many elaborate dishes and spent way too much time doing it. I'd even expended not a small amount of time and money making flower arrangements for the living room, the dining room table, the entry way, and the guest bathroom.

"That's because you're a dope," you might be saying. And as I look back and picture myself sitting there in the bathroom with the ammonia-stung eyes and the superconductor wire brush, I find I have no argument with that. But that wasn't the whole reason. The other reason I was going so far overboard to have everything, right down to the circular arrangement of the crackers in the cracker baskets, be perfect was that I was really trying to measure up to the spectacular performance of the committee member who'd been our hostess the month before. Not merely a dope, then, but a competitive dope.

I don't blame the woman who was the hostess the month before me. I'm sure she was just trying to live up to the standards set by the woman who was the hostess before her. So I asked myself, What am I doing to the poor gal, probably a competitive dope herself, who's supposed to have us all over next month?

It was very tempting at that moment to throw out all the complicated appetizers and put out a big bag of potato chips and a bowl of onion dip, if for no other reason than as a great benevolent gesture to the hostess who would follow in my footsteps. But of course I couldn't actually do that. I'd gone to far too much trouble and expense by then to just throw it all out.

And honestly, potato chips and onion dip? Who'd want to eat that? Besides me, I mean?

I didn't find out the answer that evening. But I suspect I wasn't the only committee member who would have been perfectly happy, and indeed grateful, to have been served potato chips and onion dip at the home of a friend who was nice enough to have the group over for a gathering which, after all, had one simple purpose: getting a little business done in a comfortable environment on behalf of a good cause.

Since then, I've tested that theory by asking several of my friends if they like onion dip, and they all knew exactly what I was talking about. You take an envelope of dried Lipton onion soup mix, stir it into a two-cup container of sour cream—and here's the beautiful thing: you don't even need a separate bowl—and you've got what's known as a real crowd-pleaser. In spite of admitting that they liked to eat this onion dip, however, each of my friends also said they wouldn't dream of serving it at a party. It's too low-end.

One group of people who I know for a fact are happy with not only potato chips and onion dip but also dirty toggle switches, however, are my husband and his friends. Did I say happy? Give them potato chips and onion dip and they're pigs in slop. Put out a can of smoked oysters with a side of toothpicks and it's a hoity-toity affair.

Whenever my husband has his friends over for a little get-together, I've noticed, that's about the level at which he operates. He doesn't go to anywhere near the same amount of trouble as I do, and yet they all have just as much fun. Maybe more. In fact one person who I am very certain has more fun is my husband.

He usually enjoys himself a lot more than I do when he entertains because he's not an exhausted and irritable mess by the time the people he's invited over ring the doorbell.

I know it's easy to say, "But men are just clods, clods who eat Vienna sausages on Triscuits with paper plates." It's easy to say that, and it's fun. Still, dare I suggest that this is one way in which we wives should strive to be more like our husbands? I think I will dare, because entertaining, for too many wives I know, has almost become more about impressing the guests than showing them a good time. It's become all about keeping up with expectations that always seem to get higher and higher. So I just wish we wives could get together and make a deal: I'll serve potato chips and onion dip if you will.

How wonderful it would be if we women could collectively embrace the idea of taking the level of entertaining others down a few notches. Not only would the preparations for a party be easier, but just think of how easy the cleanup would be. How long does it take to dump a potato chip bag, some oyster tins, a bunch of beer bottles, and a wad of paper napkins into a garbage pail? Sixty seconds? Whoo boy, I'd have energy left to spare! I'd have people over so much more often, because it would be easy and fun! And I could focus on the people I'd

invited—oh that's right, my *friends*, the point of the party—
instead of on getting some elaborate concoction out of the oven
every ten minutes.

If I ever sink so delightfully low, though, I'll have to be careful not to glance over at the covers of cooking magazines while
standing in the checkout line at the grocery store waiting to pay
for my Vienna sausages, because doing so would make me feel
like the most despicable slacker. I've been on photo shoots for
food before, and I've watched the food stylists in action, so part
of me knows that no food in real life ever really looks the way
it's depicted in the magazines. Sometimes it's not even edible.
Sometimes it's not even food. But it's still setting the standard
in our minds.

When you see those extraordinarily beautiful dishes in gourmet magazines and on gourmet cooking shows, it's tempting to
think that you could create them right in your own kitchen. And
certainly you could, if your kitchen were outfitted with every
professional appliance known to man, along with sixty-eight
shapes of baking tins. And definitely you could if you had a professional staff of sous chefs backing you up. And absolutely you
could if you had all merry day to do it and not another thing on
your list to worry about.

But even then I wonder if it would be worth it. For your guests, I mean. It's not necessarily a given that a chocolate cake is better, more delectable, or even more memorable if it is decorated with butter cream roses and leaves. I don't know about you, but when I see magazine pictures of really fancy food I'm not so much thinking "Yum" as I'm thinking "Wow."

In other words, it's not that I really believe the fanciest and most elaborate food would taste more delicious, it's that I believe it would make a much bigger impression on my guests. They might say I was quite the talent in the kitchen, quite the little asset to my lucky husband and family. Or at least this is what I imagine them saying as I contemplate buying the special extruder I'd need to create the butter cream flower petals.

I haven't yet purchased one of those extruders, but it's not because I'm immune from any desire to impress people, not at all. I'm vain. I'm superficial. I've already admitted I got a boob job twice. I'm just trying to honestly examine my own motivations within the context of entertaining. If I'm going to kill myself in order to show people a decent time, I would at least like to understand why.

I'm sure it's a common motivation to want to impress our guests, to have them say "Wow," and I wouldn't say that's all bad. I think what it must mean in the best light is that we want to show people that we care about them by giving them a real treat. I think it's a noble endeavor to want to treat others, and every once in a while, all of us want to be treated ourselves.

So on that note, yes, chocolate cake *is* a little more of a special treat with extruded butter cream roses than without, and I completely understand that. But what I also completely understand is that chocolate cake *without* butter cream roses is a lot more of a special treat than a package of Hostess Ding-Dongs.

Yes, like everything else, it's an issue of relativity. There's a wide spectrum, with Hostess Ding-Dongs, effortless but not exactly sensational, at one end and a chocolate cake that requires four hours to mix, bake, assemble, and then embellish, dirtying a dozen bowls and utensils in the process, at the other.

I'm not quite ready to serve Ding-Dongs for dessert at my next dinner party, but I'd love to see us all take just a step in that direction. One reason is that I want entertaining to be easier on me, yes, I admit that. But another reason is that, while I want people to enjoy my parties and also feel treated, I know that when I'm a guest in someone else's home, one thing I don't enjoy is a stressed-out hostess. I know it's a strain on my own guests, too, if they have to wonder where I am and why they keep hearing bad words coming out of the kitchen in between courses.

I think the worst party I've ever put on was for a group of my husband's friends soon after we were married, people he'd gone to school with but whom I didn't know very well. Ironically it was the party I made my biggest effort for, because I was hell-bent on impressing these four couples who were fairly new to my life.

Several days before the dinner party I started flipping through all of my cookbooks, trying to select the very best appetizer, and then the most delicious salad, and the most unusual vegetable, and the most succulent main dish, and then the most over-the-top dessert. When I finally decided on what I thought was the ideal menu, I had five or six pages of cookbooks dog-eared and I was ready to make up my shopping list, a shopping list that took up an entire page of an $8\,^1/_2$" x 11" spiral notebook.

As I look back on where things went wrong, I can see that I made two calamitous errors right at the beginning. First of all, I hadn't selected one dish that was easy and simple. I wasn't going to serve any old boiled potatoes, certainly not, but Scalloped Potatoes with Fennel, Mushrooms, and Goat Cheese would suffice. Every menu item was chosen for its "Wow" factor, without regard to ease of preparation or any familiarity I might have with

it. Which makes error number two entirely predictable: Every
menu item was one I'd never made before. I'm sure I assumed that
a dish I prepared with any regularity, even if it was time-consuming and difficult, was not good enough, simply because it was
already in my repertoire.

If you've ever done this to yourself, then you can imagine
how stressful the evening of the dinner party was for me. Being
new to each dish, I didn't know exactly how long any of them
would take me, so timing all the food to be ready at the dinner
hour was a hopeless prospect. As was any idea I'd had of depart-
ing the kitchen while the guests were arriving and settling in to
the party. My husband had to answer the door and do all the
greeting and mingling, and it was all I could do to look up from
my fully loaded cooktop, smiling a strained smile, to say hello as
the women wandered by the kitchen to see if the hostess might
be making an appearance at her own party.

"Can I help you in any way?" most of them asked, accurately
assessing the situation and feeling duly sorry for me.

"Oh, no," I called out in my happy voice each time. "Just finishing up!"

Just finishing up my social career, is what I was saying to
myself. I knew I was bombing as a hostess—I was barely in

attendance. It was too late to do anything about the overly ambitious menu, so all I could do was hope that these nice people had a good time without me.

"Did you enjoy talking to Jana?" my husband asked me later that night as we got ready for bed.

"Jana?" I looked at him wearily. "Which one was she?" All I could remember with any lucidity about the evening was how the scalloped potatoes had stayed in the oven too long and the goat cheese had separated so that the pale and mushy vegetables sat weltering in a pool of yellow grease.

Since then my wonderful friend Jana has forgiven me for trying too hard. And now when we have her and her husband over, I realize I'm better off, and so are they, if I don't try to impress them, because they're coming over to spend time with us, not to be bowled over by my attempts at being Wolfgang Puck. In fact, most often I'll ask Jana to bring a dish so I don't have to do everything myself. And I'm confident this is no imposition because I know how happy I am to bring something to her house when the tables are turned.

But I've noticed that I still go to far more trouble when I'm entertaining people I don't know very well. I suppose I feel that I can be more myself with my good friends. I know them, and I know they've come to our house for the purpose of spending time with my husband and me and the other people we've invited. I trust them to have a good time and not judge me if I'm serving the exact same simple menu I served last time.

When I think about it that way, it occurs to me that those guests I *don't* know very well would be complimented, not slighted, if I didn't go overboard, because they would know that I trusted them to be decent and gracious in the same way I trust my friends. Besides, I'm sure they don't enjoy a burned-out hostess any more than the next person.

I can't remember ever going to a party where the *host* was stressed out, by the way. And it makes me wonder, Why do we women do this to ourselves, while men don't? Why do we hold ourselves to such a high standard of performance, while men don't?

This disparity starts before we're married too. I don't know if this is true for everyone, but when I was single this is how it worked. If a single woman was asked to bring a side dish to a barbecue, she'd typically whip up something really fantastic like baked beans with green peppers, shredded Granny Smith apples, and blackstrap molasses. But if a single man was asked to bring a side dish to the same barbecue, he was likely to show up with a bucket of potato salad he purchased at the grocery store on his way over. And that was always perfectly fine. His contribution didn't raise any eyebrows; it was simply appreciated.

If a woman had done that, people would have thought, Sheesh . . . busy day, or what? We'd wonder what her excuse was for being so lame. And we'd hope that she wouldn't be too surprised if she continued to remain single, because everyone knows you don't get yourself a man that way.

"The way to a man's heart is through his stomach," the saying goes, and don't think you'll get past his gullet with some store-bought potato salad. But personally I never wanted to go in through a man's stomach—I always tried to go in through the brain. Otherwise I think women look rather shallow, scurrying around to put good vittles on the table in order to git 'hold of a man (why does the whole idea make me want to use substandard English?) and then keep aholda him by makin' sure his stomach is good 'n' full.

But then it makes men look even shallower if they are using their stomachs to think with and choosing a woman because she can cook their food.

It's obvious that's not why Michael chose me. In fact he's a good cook in his own right, and he cooks almost as many meals for our family as I do. When I cook at home, though, I've learned that I'm better off if I try to follow my mom's example and stick with what I know most of the time. Most of my childhood, my mom had a menu of seven dinners to last the week, and then she started back at the beginning. She rarely went outside of that proven plan unless there was a good reason, such as a cow that had unexpectedly died, with parts (this seems to be true of parts) that were better eaten sooner than later.

I remember going with her to the upper ranch one time, where a steer had broken its hind leg in the cattle guard. My father had taken his pistol and shot the poor animal in the fore-head, the only solution in a case like that. My mother, pragmatic and opportunistic as always, brought a big plastic bucket and a sharp knife. Stuffed beef heart was kind of a blue plate special with her, and my brothers and I had no idea that it was gross to eat heart, so we thought it was good.

By the time I got to elementary school I did find out that it was gross to have a sliced heart sandwich, because I answered with careless specificity when the person next to me asked what I was having for lunch one day. I never ate heart at school again, and it took an agonizing week for the Muffy-eats-heart talk to die down in the lunch room.

But as I said, organs were a departure—a special treat, if you will—from my mother's established menu. Since I often helped my mom with the grocery shopping, I remember how much that established menu really simplified the chore. She had a shopping list that was so standard she rarely even needed to write anything down, and she could whiz up and down the aisles picking stuff up almost without thinking. Back in the kitchen, she didn't have to worry over new recipes unless she really wanted to. Instead she perfected and mastered the recipes she knew. Seven different dinners provided variety enough both for the cook and the eaters.

Even when we had guests, even socially important guests, my mother didn't seem too worried about impressing them. From a social standpoint, I'm sure there was no one in our little valley, and perhaps many other places, more prominent than Laurance and Mary Rockefeller. They were summer residents only, but still a fixture, and although my mother and father knew them only peripherally, they were friends of my grandparents. One time my mom had them out to the ranch to have dinner with our family and my grandparents along with some ranch hands. I'm sure she prepared a good meal, but the purpose she had in mind for the food was feeding the people, not impressing them.

My mother made one of her tried-and-true dinners, and a certain egalitarian tone was set at the dinner table where family members, ranch hands, and invited guests held hands to say grace. What my mother enjoyed recounting later was that after dinner, Mr. Rockefeller stood up and carried his plate to the kitchen sink, the same as the ranch hands.

"What's he doing?" wondered Mrs. Rockefeller.

"I guess he's helping clear the table," my mother replied.

"Yes," continued the startled Mrs. Rockefeller, "but I've never seen him do that before."

I was always amazed that having these people to dinner did not change my mother's routine; just the reverse. Perhaps my mother figured that it was pointless to try and impress people who probably took their meals at the world's best restaurants on a regular basis. Or maybe she just knew that Laurance and Mary Rockefeller had the good grace to care more about fitting in with the people who were there than about what was on the menu or how it was presented. I've never made dinner for anyone socially important, in the Rockefeller sense, myself, but it helps me to think back on this episode whenever I start feeling I ought to turn myself inside out to impress visitors to our household.

Once I got over trying to impress my friends, I discovered they really are just as happy at a party where I serve a bowl of potato chips with some onion soup dip (just like my husband would with his own friends) as they are when I spend all day preparing a molded salmon mousse. So I only make the salmon mousse if I have a real hankering to make it, or to eat it.

And my friends are certainly just as happy, and just as well fed, if I don't make anything at all—if I just pick up a take-out lasagna and green salad. Actually, they're probably happier. Because in those instances I'm every bit as relaxed as they are, rather than being frazzled about last-minute preparations in some misguided effort to have everything be perfect and impressive.

But in spite of the fact that our extreme measures to "entertain" others do not necessarily add to the enjoyment of our guests, and indeed sometimes take away, the bar just seems to keep getting higher. Our cable television service provides us with an entire channel devoted to the preparation of food, and I'm not talking about onion soup dip. Sometimes it's fun to watch these shows, and in fact I've found it can be moderately addictive, just like most TV. Sometimes it's fun to imagine yourself preparing an elaborate and wonderful new dish too, or even to go ahead and give it a try. There's nothing like a cold and rainy Sunday afternoon to make me want to dabble around in the kitchen. And every once in a while, some of the shows I've watched on this channel provide ingenious shortcuts which actually make things easier.

But most of the segments are about preparing dishes that are time-consuming and difficult, and that require us to continually learn new techniques and buy ever more specialized cooking tools. It's easy to forget that these people on television are operating on both a professional level and in a video-edited timeframe, neither of which can be achieved in our real lives. And this is especially true when the focus is on entertaining, because the assumption is that when you're having non-family members for dinner, they might as well be the Rockefellers, and it's reason enough to go far, far beyond what you would normally do.

Now we have all kinds of celebrities following in the steps of Martha Stewart and offering up their own books on how to throw a really perfect party. Never mind that these celebrities don't actually have to do any of the work for their parties in real life, they'll show us how to make every gathering the most elegant, the most lavish, the most grand for our guests.

Last time I looked, Amazon's Web site had more than fifty books with the words "Perfect Party" in the title. You'll only find a couple of matches when you search for books that have "Fun Party" in the title, though, if you don't count the ones for children. This little research project might be unscientific, but it provides a startling perspective on what our priorities might be when it comes to entertaining. Do we want things to be perfect or fun?

I know that sometimes entertaining in a fancy way can be fun, even for the hostess. Everyone should do it when they enjoy it. But sometimes it helps me to be reminded that the whole point of entertaining is the people who will be there, not the lengths I could go to to impress them.

What I've gathered by skimming through the Perfect Party books is that any dinner party can be approached as though it's a wedding. The seating arrangements, the invitations, the music selection, the floral theme—these are all issues which we can make a big deal over before we even begin to discuss the food. We can even turn a picnic into a complicated and ostentatious affair if we allow ourselves.

But I don't want to allow myself, because I don't think it sounds all that fun. I don't think any of my parties need to be perfect, and what I've learned the hard way is that my guests don't really enjoy themselves when I'm a frazzled wretch, no matter how hard I might try not to let on.

I realize that might sound like a self-serving rationale for underperforming as a wife and hostess. But that doesn't mean it's not true.

chapter 5

Doing less and loving it

I remember one year after my husband and I got married receiving a Christmas card from a college friend of his who was still single.

"That's Millard for you," said Michael. "He's got his own set of china too."

I never met Mr. Millard, and I'm sure he's a nice person, but I did have to side with my husband that it seemed a little different for a single man to be sending out holiday greeting cards. Usually a man waits until he gets married to do that sort of thing, and even then he doesn't do it because it's the wife's job.

At least it always has been in our family. About five years ago I dropped the ball on our holiday greeting cards and didn't get them done, but do you think my husband stepped in and did them for me? No. People simply didn't hear from us that year, and I'm sure they didn't say "That lazy Mike" to themselves.

It's also been the wife's job, in our family as in most other families I know, to write all the thank-you notes and sympathy cards, to send out any birth announcements and party invitations, to respond to invitations from others, and to buy and send all the birthday presents and wedding gifts, even if they're going to far-flung relatives of the husband's whom the wife has never actually met.

For the most part these tasks and their completion have been pretty much invisible to my husband. Although I do remember one time when Michael was taken by surprise at his office to be thanked by a colleague of his for a wedding gift.

"Wow, honey," he said when he got home, "the Breinholts really liked their towels. Thanks for making me look so good."

"No problem," I replied, "but next time you say that I'd appreciate it if you placed more emphasis on *look*."

It's one thing to look good, but I was the one actually *doing* all those good deeds. And I wondered why I always had to be the social director for both of us. What is this, I asked myself, The Olden Days?

In The Olden Days it was a wife's job to make her husband look good from a social standpoint at all times. She maintained social connections not only on her own behalf, but on her husband's behalf too. In fact, the wife was actually supposed to add social credence to her husband in order to advance his career. And the really quaint thing is that I think it actually worked.

In the 1950s a man stood a better chance of getting a pro-
motion at the office if his wife promoted him outside the office,
with lots of civic and social involvement of her own. The sooner she got to be president of the gardening club, the sooner he
could be president of the company. If the wife made nice with
all the other wives in the company, the husband's own peers
would like him better. If she had his boss over to dinner and the
pork roast didn't go up in flames, then hopefully neither would
his job.

But this isn't the 1950s and I don't have time to keep up my
own social status, much less my husband's, partly because I'm
working at a job just like he is. So I decided a few years ago to
stand right up for myself and to foist the function of social correspondent off on my husband for a change. See how he liked it.

I handed him a stack of invitations and said, "Here. *You* call
all these people and RSVP. *You* arrange for babysitters on all
these nights. *You* go out and buy birthday presents for all these
three-year-olds. *I'm* not doing it."

"Neither am I," said Michael as he leafed through the stack.

"Hrrk!" I responded, unable to come up with an actual word.

"I don't really want to go to any of these things," Michael
continued. "So let's just call them up and say no."

What? You can't just say no, even Nancy Reagan knows that now. You've got to have a multimillion-dollar advertising campaign telling you how to say no, showing you that life will go on if you do say no, demonstrating that lots of other people are saying no but they still look cool. Otherwise you can't do it, you can't just simply say no.

But it dawned on me that my husband truly had no problem with it, so I grabbed the stack of invitations back as fast as I could. When he said, "Let's just call them up and say no," he meant me anyway.

So my strategy had backfired in more ways than one. I had not succeeded in proving to Michael how difficult the job of social correspondent was, but even more disturbing, I'd also realized that I was probably the one who'd turned it into such a big job. And I started to wonder, Why is it that he can say no and I can't seem to? My friends say the same thing about their husbands too. They say no to things more easily than the wives do.

This is true not only when it comes to social engagements, but with so many other commitments my friends and I tend to get in over our heads with, schedulewise. Volunteer work. Joining committees. Helping out at school. Selling tickets to stuff. For some reason it seems quite difficult for us to say, "No, I'm sorry, I can't do it. I can't be there." I'm not sure why this is. Perhaps we women are just nicer. Perhaps the piggish male of the species is innately more self-centered and therefore less likely to go out of his way just to please other people when it's not strictly necessary.

That sounds like a compelling theory; I know I enjoyed coming up with it. But maybe it's not the right one. Maybe men can say no more easily because they're simply more confident than we women are. Maybe they feel that they have less to prove. And maybe I wouldn't blame them if they did. Because if you lined up all the history books that have been written about men—men and the countries they've founded or conquered, men and the great new gadgets they've invented, men and the ingenious ideas they've thought up—it would take up a tad more shelf space than a similar selection about women.

So it wouldn't be too surprising if men, who for centuries have been better educated, better funded, and provided with more opportunities and high-tech equipment than we women have been, think they're already making enough of a contribution without constantly being derailed by the addition of new activities. It wouldn't be too surprising if they were more certain of their social value. And it shouldn't be a big shock to us then if they didn't feel that they had to continually reestablish their value by saying yes to all the things they're asked to do.

We women, though, tend to be pleasers. A lot of us just like to make people happy, if not outright save them. If you combine that rescuer mentality with an ongoing need to prove ourselves and earn social acceptance, it might start to explain why too many women I know say yes to too many things and end up over-loaded, with too much to do in too many areas of their lives: work, family, church, charity, and social engagements.

But it also seems that we women are asked to do things more often than men are asked. Especially when it comes to certain kinds of volunteer work. My husband knows his way around a kitchen, for instance, but has anyone ever asked him to bring in a basket of brownies for a grade-school bake sale? Oh, that'll be the day. He's not even put in the position of saying yes or no to that. Yet somehow I would find I'd consented to bringing in brownies without even realizing it.

"You didn't consent, you volunteered!" is how the committee head would explain it.

"I did? When?"

"At our last meeting."

"But I wasn't at your last meeting." Oh, now I see.

This kind of thing doesn't happen to my husband, though, and it makes me wonder if people might view a woman's time as more expendable.

It makes me wonder if there's a perception that women, even women who have households to run, children to raise, and/or paying jobs to go to, have more choices about what to do with their time than men do. And that furthermore, what women might be doing, even when they're busy, is not as essential as what men are doing, so interruptions of their schedule will have lesser consequences than the same interruption of a man's schedule. I think this is especially true for so-called stay-at-home moms. Maybe that's why so many of the ones I know are busier and more frazzled than anyone else.

I work an erratic schedule these days, so I'm not solicited as much as stay-at-home moms, but more than friends who work full-time. Actually, I don't mind being asked. For one thing, I know that volunteer workers are essential to so many organizations, and some of them are organizations that benefit me and my family. I also know how hard it is to round up help.

But I've found that I don't do anybody any good when I take on more than I can adequately accomplish. I just end up resenting my commitments and kicking myself for making them. I never

intentionally overload my schedule, but sometimes it sneaks up
on me. Taken one at a time, everything I agree to participate in
seems to have some merit, at least in the moment, but they add up
so quickly. There came a point in my life several years ago when
I couldn't even remember what I was supposed to be doing on
any given day without first consulting my Palm Pilot.

I actually got so dependent on it that I would check it before
I even got out of bed in the morning. Had to make sure that was
on the schedule for the day. It had taken over my life, the little
rectangle, and was telling me what to do. Oh, I knew that technically I was telling myself what to do. Technically. I realized the
fiendish machine didn't actually make entries to the calendar
without my having wielded the stylus at some point. But I often
did wonder how so many commitments, and certain ones in particular, got on there.

I think the biggest problem with my life-according-to-Palm-
Pilot days was not even the number of commitments, though. It
was the lack of prioritizing. The absence of thoughtful discrimina-
tion. Looking back it seems as though it got to the point where
the most important criterion for whether or not I added an obligation to my schedule had become whether or not there was
space on the agenda. Well, I've got nothing else at five o'clock, so

99

all-righty then. You could probably have asked me to show up at a cock fight, and as long as it was taking place during an available time segment, I'd have said yes.

I'm sure that, once I looked at the Palm Pilot and saw what it had on the schedule for the day, I would have been able to drum up some flu-like symptoms to get out of actually going to the cock fight. But knowing me, I would have felt guilty too.

I have a rather feeble ego, I suppose. I am not only susceptible to guilt, but I am easily made to feel that I can't say no because there will be no one who can quite replace me and my extraordinary talents if I do. I know that's another reason why it used to be so easy to keep adding more to my calendar when what I really needed to be doing was taking things off.

But I'm getting better at taking things off my schedule all the time. I'm not only saying no myself these days, I'm recommending it to friends. I'm doing less, for a change, instead of more and more and more.

I achieved a milestone in this regard a while back when I resigned from my position as Vice-Chair of a nonprofit board for a botanical garden. I care about this organization and I think it makes our city a better place. I also care about keeping my word. But I knew that in six months' time when I became Chair of their board, I wouldn't be able to do a good job. Although accepting this position had been a commitment I'd made in good faith, it was no longer a commitment I could keep and do any justice to.

At the time I'd made it, two years prior, I hadn't had nearly as much on my plate, primarily because my career in advertising had really been on the back burner. Since then, things had changed quite considerably. In fact I was beginning a new career as a writer, and I'd made it a high priority to succeed at whatever level I could. But I knew I wouldn't succeed if I didn't devote the requisite time, which was tantamount to a full-time job. And I still wanted to spend as much time as possible with my husband and kids. So after weighing the options, I called the Executive Director to tell him of my decision, and that we needed to find someone else.

"Why, you lazy, no-account, little traitor," or something along those lines, was the response I was ready for. But that's not what he said. He was nice enough to act disappointed, but he was also smart enough to have seen this coming and was actually waiting for me to arrive at the same conclusion he'd already reached. Furthermore, since he'd been anticipating that I would need to bow out, he'd been mulling over some ideas for someone to succeed me and anticipated that it would be "no problem."

101

Say what?

"Oh, right," I had to remind myself out loud. "That's good. I'm *happy* about that." I might bring something unique to the table, but so does the next person. The organization I care about will continue to move forward with new ideas and fresh effort, even if they don't come from me.

But some days later I was telling a colleague about the episode and was reminded that, as usual, I seem to be in the minority.

"You must feel horrible," she sympathized.

"No, not really," I said.

"But it's got to be hard to feel like you're a quitter," she pointed out. "And even if you're not one, you don't want to look like one either."

"But I don't think I'm—"

"And what's worse," she added, "is that now you'll have to wonder if you'll ever be asked to do anything again."

"Well," I tried to interject, "I would hope—"

"But even if you're not, so what?" she concluded. "If you can't do it, you can't do it."

"You're right," I said, and decided to leave it at that.

I perceived that this exchange was supposed to have thoroughly convinced me of my own pathetic lameness. She didn't go so far as to tell me I was making my husband look bad, but other than that she'd managed to voice the exact fears that cause so many of us to say "Yes!" and "Absolutely!" and "I'm your woman!" to every opportunity that comes our way.

But I didn't feel lame. I felt good about having taken an obligation off my plate that I truly did not have time for, and I only wished that this overscheduled, overcompetitive, and overstressed woman could start smoking the same thing I'd been smoking.

I was also glad to have been reminded by the whole episode that I am replaceable. And that just because I care about something doesn't mean I need to personally see to it that it is put to bed in the manner that I and only I can achieve. In fact, there are probably lots of things which might end up on my list that actually don't need to be done at all.

I once worked for a company whose CEO deliberately managed every department so that all the employees were assigned too many duties, to the point where no one was able to do all the things that were included in their job description, and for which they'd been told they'd be held responsible. Unfortunately this made some of the more fastidious people's heads explode, but the rest of us coped the only way we could. By forcing ourselves to carefully scrutinize all our responsibilities, to prioritize them, and to let some of them go undone.

It might sound as though that CEO was just callously conducting a little social experiment, but I think he was probably correct if he figured those individuals doing the work would be in the best position to decide which specific tasks were truly important. And perhaps he had the uncommon insight to know that not everything is. Maybe he understood that just because something was on your todo list didn't, by definition, mean it was worth committing the time needed to actually get it done.

I learned from that experience, and my head never quite blew into bits. I've also realized that it's every bit as important for me to prioritize tasks now that I'm not working for that same company. I was single then, and when I think back to my time as their employee, I don't remember having nearly as many things in my job description then as I do now, now that I'm a working wife and a mom.

Oh, I'm sure I could be more efficient. But ultraefficiency is something I balk at, and don't even talk to me about multitasking. Blech. Of course we wives and moms have to get used to doing a bunch of things at once. But it's easy to take on way too many of them by characterizing it with positive sounding words such as "multitasking" and "efficiency." It reminds me of the time another of my employers thought it would be a good idea for me and some

other managers to get up and running with time management software. This was going to bring order, they promised, to my chaotic
schedule by making me super efficient.

But I quickly discovered that it was going to take quite a bit
of time out of my schedule to figure out how to operate the application they'd installed on my computer. And then I would have
to go through a pretty steep learning curve to get to the point
where I was using the software to its best advantage.

And I immediately began to suspect that I did not want to
use the software to its best advantage. First I was supposed to go
through a tutorial so I could understand where I was "losing"
time, which would lead to suggestions on how I could "gain" time.
From that exercise, I gathered that I was spending far too much
time thinking and should cut that out.

In any case, as I perused the materials I realized that time
management software was not going to help me in the way I
wanted to be helped, because it wasn't going to take anything off
my list.

Just the opposite—it was going to put more things on my list
by making me more organized and efficient, helping me make sure
that I did not "waste" one moment of my time by not ever having
a space on my calendar with nothing on it, otherwise known as

"unproductive time." So I told my employer I was absolutely planning to get started with the time management software in the future but at the present I did not have time, and yes, I did think I was funny.

Now I'm out of the corporate world, but it doesn't mean I've escaped this managing-your-time-for-maximum-productivity mentality. Not at all. Most women I know, like myself, have too many things to do if they are wives and moms. This breed is commonly known as the juggler, and it seems you can always throw one more buzzing chainsaw into the fray.

I realize that right now some people, thinking along the lines of my previous employer, might suggest that women like me are just big whiners who need to stop complaining and simply get ourselves organized. But again, I'm not at all sure that being more efficient and organized is always the answer. Organization can be a positive thing, but I'm not sure it's always the solution to chaos.

There's a new industry in our country called Stuff Management. This industry is comprised of people and products that help you sort and organize the hundreds of possessions you've accumulated but can't seem to "manage." Or even, sometimes, find. The majority of these possessions will not be ones you actually use, of course, because most of the solutions provided by the Stuff Management business have to do with storage.

I've read articles about the extraordinary growth being experienced by this industry and have wondered if anybody's asking what seems to be the obvious question: Why do we have so much stuff in the first place? Wouldn't it be easier to just get rid of half of it rather than managing it all? Or hiring someone to manage it for us?

I feel similarly about the items on my schedule. Some might say I need to get my schedule more organized, but I can tell you that it works even better sometimes just to take certain things off it. I envision this as an exciting new form of time management called Highlight & Delete. And I think, as an industry, that it could potentially achieve the same kind of growth (or would it be shrinkage?) as Stuff Management.

I know it's important to accomplish things, and I'm not just talking about things that are easy. I also think it's important to do your best to keep your commitments, even if it becomes inconvenient to do so. And I think that work in general is important, and that sometimes even productivity is a commendable goal, if productivity means you changed things for the better.

But busy and productive are two different things.

Maybe this is as good a time as any to notify my friends and family that one word I'd rather not be used to describe me in my obituary is the word "busy." I don't want to be remembered as someone who hustled and bustled through life. I wouldn't mind the term "hard worker." If someone wanted to say "multitalented," that would be fine. But those traits are different from being busy-busy-busy.

In fact I wouldn't be upset, or come back to haunt you in any way, if my obituary actually said, "She seemed to have an inordinate amount of free time."

For the women I know, and—what the hell—maybe even for the men, free time needs to be a higher priority. Free time is something we should have in abundance in our wealthy country, but we don't because we are too busy. We're so appalled at the idea of wasting our time that we've actually become adept at simply looking busy, even when we have nothing to do.

Maybe that's why even when we schedule free time, it's often not what you would call "free." On our vacations, many of us truly believe we can see the entire West Coast of the United States in a week. Europe in ten days? Merely a trifle. But what a nutty one. You could maybe see the island of Sardinia in ten days. By the time we get home from these whirlwind tours, we are

exhausted, bewildered, and the opposite of relaxed, but hey—
we've had a fabulous vacation! A break from "work"! And just
think how industrious and productive we were—just think how
much we got done. Italy? Check. Spain? Check. Germany?
Double check.

This ambitious vacation style can partly be chalked up to the
fact that American vacations are simply too short. We don't give
ourselves enough time to really wind down, whereas Europeans,
by contrast, often take vacations (or "holidays," which sounds even
more fun) that last a month or more. And they sometimes check
into a hotel and don't check out the entire time, the slackers.

I don't know about anybody else, but to me that sounds like
a civilized way of vacationing. These people, these Europeans
who somehow get away with doing this, don't have to pack and
unpack the whole time they're on vacation. They don't have to
continually reorient themselves, figuring out on a daily basis how
to get where they're going, where to have dinner, what currency
they're now supposed to be using. They have the time to really
soak up their surroundings, perhaps make friends, maybe even
begin to feel at home in a different part of the world.

And what's amazing is that these workers are taking all this
time off with the actual blessing of their employers, who are

taking the same lengthy vacations *themselves*, and yet somehow their business gets done, somehow their national economies don't come screeching to a halt.

I want to be in their club. Then again, they probably wouldn't have me. For one thing, I've never even taken a month-long vacation. But I will say that one of the best vacations our family's ever had was a vacation we canceled. We were supposed to go to California for five days to visit numerous relatives of my husband's, but plans changed at the last minute on their end and we ended up staying home. The beauty of the situation was that we hadn't planned on being at home so we had nothing—absolutely nothing—on our calendar for five whole days.

Not only were we spared the madcap tour of northern California, trying to make all the rounds between parents, siblings, uncles, and nephews in a blur of barbecues and traffic jams, but we were also spared the typical hubbub associated with five days at home. All of our friends thought we were on our trip, so we received virtually no phone calls.

My husband and I took a bona fide breather, and didn't realize until afterwards how sorely we'd needed it. We actually had the time to catch up with each other in a more than superficial way. We had wonderfully lengthy conversations, something we hadn't been able to do for a long time. We caught up with our kids too, and were able to play with them in a lazy, free-associating kind of way, where one thing just led to another if you wanted it to, and everybody seemed to be doing what they enjoyed doing.

But we realized that that blissful stretch of five days with "nothing" to do was something that could only have happened by accident, and we asked ourselves why that was. As much as our whole family, and all of us individually, had benefited from this truly free time, we wondered why we didn't place a higher premium on it. Why, when we set our priorities, did free time never make it onto our to-do list? Why did we only enjoy it by default?

Perhaps it's because in a culture that promotes and admires busy-ness, having nothing in particular that you're obligated to do feels like the most delinquent pleasure. So if you really want to make free time an important priority, you have to get to the point where you don't feel like a big loser if, when someone asks what you're planning on doing for the coming weekend, you sometimes answer, "Not a thing."

That's easier said than done, because admitting that we have no plans, nothing to do, feels foreign to so many of us. And I mean that literally, because it almost feels un-American. Our country is the leader of the industrialized world, and the assumption is we got there by being extremely industrious (although I'd like to put a plug in for inventiveness and creativity).

What's worse for us women, though, it that doing nothing feels even more unseemly for a wife than it does for her husband. Has anyone ever seen a cartoon drawing of a wife loafing in a backyard hammock, a newspaper over her face and a can of beer on her stomach? It's difficult to even produce that picture in your mind's eye, and if you succeed it's quite bizarre. But the husband loafing in the hammock is a visual we see all the time. It's as well-known a cliché as Dagwood Bumstead loafing on the couch. I'm not even sure our society looks down on him for doing it either, because we probably assume that he's entitled, given all he's contributing the rest of the time.

By that measure it might be Blondie and the rest of us women who should be wearing out the couch cushions. But first we'd have to stop feeling guilty, because otherwise we wouldn't get any good shuteye.

I don't get as many naps as I'd really like to get, myself. But I have given myself emotional permission to take a break, and it's been quite rejuvenating. Now that I'm comfortable bowing out of certain activities, my job as social director is much easier too. And the job of social correspondent is also easier, because my husband is doing his part.

Michael spent a week in the hospital a few years ago with a heart condition—a rather large scare for us both—and received a number of gift baskets, plants, and flower arrangements from friends. I kept a list of the senders, and after he was out of the hospital and out of the woods healthwise, I intended to sit down and write notes to everyone.

But then I thought, Wait—what do I write? Thank you for your thoughtfulness, my husband is doing much better, but not quite well enough to write this note? He was well enough to go to work, so I determined that he could write his own thank you notes too. When I gave him the list of recipients he didn't say, "Can't you do this?" He said, "Thank you." And shortly started addressing envelopes.

Wow. Perhaps next year I might give him our Christmas card list. If Mr. Millard could do it, I'm sure Mr. Ferro could too.

chapter 6

Joined in matrimony,
just not at the hip

-6-

In the first few months after Michael and I got married, I remember asking his permission one time to go out and have dinner on a Saturday evening with a gang of my girlfriends. He stood there and looked at me like I'd just announced my intention to shave my head.

"What's the matter with you?" he asked.

Fortunately, I was unarmed. All I could do was commence a tirade about all the times he went out with his own dumb friends when he continued, "You don't need my permission. Just go ahead and go."

Oh. Thank goodness I wasn't too far into the tirade.

"Okay," I said. "I was just, uh, letting you know, and your friends aren't dumb."

An adroit save, but I knew they were two different things. It was ordinary courtesy to let him know of my plans, but he was right that I didn't need to seek his permission. I was a grown woman. What in the world was I doing, asking him if I could have his okay? What *was* the matter with me?

I'll tell you what the matter was. The matter was that I had mentally prepared myself, when I got married, to subordinate all my other relationships to the one I had with my husband. I'd had other close friends who'd as good as dropped off the face of the earth once they got married, and I assumed that my own friendships would also have to suffer, now that I'd found The One.

But while one is an ample number as far as husbands go, it's not nearly enough as far as close relationships go. Besides, I've always found that a man I'm close to is no substitute for a woman I'm close to. I would have been a miserable wretch if I'd let my other friendships go by the wayside, and I know Michael doesn't want to be married to someone who's a miserable wretch. He tried that the week after I gave birth to Belle and it didn't suit him.

I do place a lot more importance, relatively speaking, on my marriage and family than on my relationships with girlfriends. But intimate relationships with family members and with outside friends are not mutually exclusive, and I seem to require both.

This hasn't appeared to undermine my marriage. In fact, from my perspective as a wife, I can testify that a person who has numerous healthy relationships outside their marriage is a more interesting person to be married to. One of the most attractive things about my husband is that so many other people like him and enjoy him and want to be around him. So the fact that he's involved in lots of meaningful relationships outside our marriage makes him more desirable, not less. It makes him a better husband, not a worse one.

Since we both had good friends when we met, spousal blessing has never been part of the criteria for either of us for the friends we select or spend time with. I really do enjoy Michael's friends, though. It's just too bad my husband's not writing this book for a minute so he could say, "And I enjoy your friends." Oh well, I have to speak for him, not that I have any qualms.

In fact now that I've vicariously given him the floor, I'm sure he wouldn't stop there. "You're an interesting person to be married to as well," he would add, "and your relationships outside our marriage make you even more desirable too."

An eloquent man. And I'm confident he'd also agree that my friendships deserve my time and attention on a regular basis, just like his do, even if it "takes away" from the time I spend with my husband and kids.

Speaking of kids, it's probably even easier to think you should devote yourself exclusively to your children rather than to your husband. They need you more. But I would go nuts if I

didn't have other moms to talk to, and I know it's made me a better parent to have close friendships with other mothers,
especially those who have kids near the same age as mine. As a
mom I get frustrated, confused, and overwhelmed at times with
the surprises and the dilemmas of bringing up kids, and at those
times it's invaluable and it's comforting to have another mom to
compare notes and stories with. Maybe even more so for someone like myself who doesn't have her own mom to turn to.

I remember worrying about my little boy a few years ago in
a way that seems foolish to me now. I'm very glad, in retrospect,
that I decided to confide in my sympathetic and levelheaded
friend Julie before sending Joe straight off to a child psychologist.

"I don't know what to do about Joe," I told her, "because he
just loves matches, and candles, and fire."

"So does Ian!" she exclaimed. Her Ian is about the same age
as Joe. "What is it with these boys?"

"I don't know," I continued, "but I've just read that most juvenile delinquents had a history of setting fires when they were
little. So I'm really not sure what to do."

Now maybe I shouldn't have imparted that to her, since it
sounded like her little boy was headed for the clink along with
mine, but we launched into a dialogue on the subject. And as we

talked, she remembered how her brothers had been enthralled with fire when they were little, and I recollected that the same had been true of my own brothers. And that, actually, it had been true of me.

Fire was no big deal when I was growing up because it was a practical tool in our ranch operation. We didn't have trash pick-up back then, so we incinerated all our garbage in a pair of old oil drums. Excess lumber generated by torn-down sheds or fences was deposited in the dump we had in the gully across the road from our house, and it was one of the great thrills of my early life when my mom and dad decided it was time to burn it all up. We had giant bonfires in the wintertime, with flames shooting to thirty feet, and these were occasions for lots of people to gather round; family, ranch hands, and neighbors.

But my brothers and I saw that accidental fires had the same destructive power as the ones you set on purpose. Our haystacks at that time were just twenty-ton piles of loose hay with a slat fence around the bottom, and if the hay hadn't been dried thoroughly enough before being stacked, it could begin to decompose in the middle, a heat-generating process which sometimes caused the entire stack to actually combust from the inside out. On a more spectacular note, our calving barn burned down one morning in

the space of twenty minutes after a freshly branded and disorient-
ed calf bolted from the branding chute. The calf ran over the
propane heater for the branding irons and disconnected the hose,
which then spewed lit fuel erratically onto the side of the barn like
a blowtorch. It went up like paper.

Perhaps those fire stories seem like a departure from my
point about my relationship with Julie and how much it helps me
as a parent. But I make the departure partly to illustrate one of
the things I most appreciate about her. She's willing to go where
the conversation takes us and never suggests that we get back "on
point." Sometimes just having the conversation is the point. Julie
had some fire stories of her own to tell me, and I think we probably gabbed about it for more than an hour.

As we traded tales, we eventually worked our way back to
the point anyway. We agreed that both Ian and Joe would eventually come to understand the complex nature of something that's
both a great danger and a useful tool, the same way we'd grown
to understand that as kids. And we agreed that it would be kind
of weird if kids didn't find fire fascinating, because it is in fact fascinating. And that just because our little boys were interested in
fire didn't automatically mean they'd burn up all our possessions
and then move on to grand theft auto.

I came away from that lengthy and engrossing discussion with my friend feeling a great deal better. I wasn't planning to leave Joe all alone with an Aim 'n' Flame, but thanks to Julie I was confident as a mom that I could teach him about fire—the good and the bad—and I had to laugh at myself for having drawn a conclusion from something that for all I knew was a statistical coincidence and not necessarily relevant to Joe either way.

It's true that I might have had just the same outcome by discussing the topic with my husband. But it wasn't solely the outcome that was significant to me. It was the process. My husband doesn't have it in him to worry about our children the way I do, much less discuss it at great length. Nine times out of ten when I go to him and say, "I'm worried about Joe," he'll respond with some version of, "Don't be."

I'm sorry, that doesn't do it for me. His advice might turn out to be correct in the end, but that's not sufficient. He just doesn't have the patience to dig in and debate personal issues the way my girlfriends are willing to, much less to take off on tangents about decomposing haystacks right in the middle of the discussion. My friends and I might reach the same conclusion our husbands would, but we don't just leap right to it. We chew on it, test it, circle around it, and are willing to talk about it at great length without looking at our watches.

I hope this won't be an unpleasant surprise to any of my husband's friends, by the way, but I must say that he usually looks at his watch when he's talking to them on the phone. I've never seen him talk on the phone for more than three or four minutes without checking the time. But I don't suppose his friends would be offended, because they don't want to yap any longer than Michael does anyway. I, on the other hand, can talk on the phone with a friend for an hour or more without even realizing how much time has passed by. And I truly think that if sleep were not a biological necessity, I could sit and jaw with particular friends of mine in person and not stop for days.

Michael readily agrees with me that men and women conduct their relationships differently, but of course in his mind men conduct them in a superior fashion. One time he told me he believes that women get so mired in each other's personal details, nonverbal nuances, and exact choice of words—always looking for the unspoken intention, always taking everything seriously—that they'll sacrifice a friendship over any insignificant perceived insult. Over incidental piffling jealousies. Over an unreturned sweater.

"What kind of sweater?" I inquired.

But he didn't laugh. He didn't even appreciate that I was being witty and funny. I couldn't believe that was truly his perception, of me or of my friends! Hmmph. What my husband might not realize is that it's never about the sweater. It's always more complicated than that, more layered. There's a history there, I can guarantee him.

I admit my women friends and I take things more personally; we're more personally involved. We know more about each other because we talk about everything. Maybe, sometimes, we know too much. But I'd rather conduct my friendships on a somewhat substantial and meaningful plane than select my best friend based on the fact that he owns the same kind of fly rod.

Say! I believe I just got back at my husband for the sweater remark.

I'm sure he'll forgive me, though, because he doesn't envy my friendships. He prefers his own. And he's probably right that they're easier and simpler. On the other hand, I love the fact that my friends and I are willing to devote some real time to deliberating things and don't care if my husband wonders why we have to "beat everything to death." I also have to point out that I know quite a bit more about what's going on with my friends than he does with his, especially when it comes to personal details. And sometimes, through their wives, I also know more about what's going on with *his* friends than he does. I might ask him, for example, "How's so-and-so doing?"

And Michael will answer, "Fine. Why?"

"Well, he just got a vasectomy. I wondered how he was handling it."

"What? He got a vasectomy?"

I'm sure part of the reason I'm usually better informed about this type of thing is the simple fact that I can talk longer. But it's also because I tend to cement my relationships with others in one-on-one situations, in which it's easier to talk intimately, whereas my husband seems to prefer groups.

In fact, last summer my husband reached what was for him a fun little anniversary because he attended his twentieth consecutive BWO. That's an acronym for Boys' Weekend Out, an annual excursion he goes on with his old Sigma Chi friends from college. They do give the term "weekend" rather generous parameters, I discovered when we were dating, because he's typically gone for five days. He does it every year and has the twenty different T-shirts to prove it.

That's right, these buddy-boys make such a big production out of their annual time to get drunk and talk loud and basically undergo their version of bonding that one of them who's a graphic designer actually comes up with a new BWO logo every year. And then they have custom T-shirts made so they can all wear the same thing while they're attending Boys' Weekend Out and feel even more like they're members of the same platoon.

Or, I don't know, maybe it's so no one gets lost. But either way, the whole thing just makes a wife want to say, "C'mon, boys! This isn't college! You're not in a fraternity anymore! Let it go!"

Cripes. I have to be honest, though. When I first found out about the Boys' Weekend Out thing, back when Michael and I were dating, I didn't so much want to say, "Let it go," as I wanted to say, "Can I go?"

I felt jealous, actually, because my girlfriends and I don't do big annual trips like that. I knew I'd never be invited on Boys' Weekend. So my response to my initial feelings of envy was to announce to my future husband that if he really thought he was going to carry on this tradition throughout our marriage, then I was jolly well going to do the same thing. I figured that right before we tied the knot was a good time to spring some ultimatums on him.

"Go ahead," he said.

"Oh, I will," I said.

"Fine," he said.

"Fine," I said.

So that backfired, then. He didn't care if I did do the same thing. But then I took a moment and visualized myself getting twenty women together for an annual trek through, say, the southern Utah desert. And certainly the Utah desert has its own compelling appeal, but getting twenty women together? Organizing them? Rounding them up every morning to go on a hike, knowing they'll want to jibber-jabber the whole time?

Ick. Book club is much more my speed.

What I really wanted to say to Michael was not that I wanted to do the same thing he does, but that my friendships were just as important to me as his were to him. Actually, I don't want to do the same thing with my friends that he does with his, and I don't want to go with him when he goes.

The truth is that at this point, eight years into our marriage, when Michael walks out the door with his fishing rod and duffle bag to go off for five days with twenty of his friends, the word I would use to describe what I genuinely feel is not "jealousy." It's more like "jubilation."

I love the man and I know I'll miss him, but shout hallelujah, once he's backed his car down the driveway and off the property, I know I've got five whole days at home with just myself and kids. Five days of reading my novel late into the night with a box of rice crackers on my lap if I want it. Five days of leaving my bras and panties and T-shirts strewn around the bedroom floor and chair backs. This, at least on a temporary basis, is bliss.

Perhaps everyone gets to the point in their marriage, no matter how infatuated with each other they once were, when they realize they have no need or desire to spend every breathing moment together. I know Michael and I don't have to be joined at the hip to still be in love. We do love each other and we love our times together, but we're not obsessed with each other or emotionally dependent on each other.

A friend of mine got engaged last year, and she and her fiancé realized as they discussed how to approach the sale of their respective houses that they'd probably be better off if they didn't sell them. They'd be happier as a couple if they continued to maintain two small houses rather than consolidating into one larger one. And so that's what they've done. They're almost always together at one house or the other, but they were both in their forties when they entered into their marriage, and they knew themselves well enough to know that they sometimes like to be alone. Need to be alone. Will tear each other limb from limb if they aren't permitted to be alone. For them, their time alone makes their time together far better.

What they've chosen to do is kind of like the concept behind twin beds, only with houses. I know twin beds for married couples are probably even less common these days than two houses but they used to be pretty popular, and I think I'm beginning to understand their appeal. Michael and I don't have twin beds, partly because our bedroom is very narrow and partly because we sometimes think it's fun to have the whole family in one bed, including the dogs.

But if my husband ever suggested that we change to twin beds, I'd certainly consider it. First of all, it would mean I'd no longer have to make his bed just because I was making mine. That's something right there. But more important, I don't think it would separate us in any significant way. If we wanted to be together, then we could really be together. In other words, we could roll around together in a cozy little twin bed. But if we wanted to sleep, we could go for broke in that way too, and sleep alone so we could get some really first-rate rest.

That's the way I look at the friendships both Michael and I have outside our marriage. The fact that we're not together all the

time doesn't ultimately separate us, because it puts more value
and emphasis on the times when we are.

I should add that my friendships outside my marriage aren't
limited to women, though. I also have male friends whom I love
and rely on, even though they aren't any more keen on beating
things to death than my husband is. My business partner,
Steve, for instance. I've worked with him on and off for nearly fifteen years, and it's a relationship that sustains me in a way
no other relationship does. Although we're friends, more than
just colleagues, our social lives are almost completely separate.
I rarely see him outside the office. We've never dated. I don't
really know his family well, and he doesn't know mine except
casually.

And yet, in an essential compartment of my life, I'm as close
to him as I am to anyone else. He's a graphic designer and I'm a
copywriter, and for many years we've worked as a team on advertising projects. I rarely do advertising work these days, so now
we're office mates and company for one another at lunch time
more than anything else. But my work as a writer is about my
ideas, and Steve is still the person I most often consult with to get
an honest read on whether or not my ideas hold water for anyone except me.

We developed a very frank way of communicating with each
other a long time ago, out of professional necessity in a business
of deadlines, and we both know we can count on the other person to tell us if we're on track or off. There's not a lot of
pussyfooting and there's no being charitable, because clarity is
more important. We've spent so much time together over the past
fifteen years that he knows me very well, and I think I know him.
I also trust him and I trust his judgment. Steve's the one who told
me, for example, that I should definitely not title this chapter
"Why Women Are Superior," and I did listen to him.

Which reminds me, the other thing that can be so helpful
about being friends with a man is that it provides a man's perspective on things, even sometimes on the topic that men seem to
dread the most: relationships. Sometimes my male friends serve to
remind me that male creatures as a whole are wired differently
than we women, they just are. My husband is not necessarily a
freak of nature, in other words.

And sometimes, I must admit, the way men are wired actually
works better. Women are not inherently superior, just as Steve said.
I remember one time that my friend Charlie was listening to my
friend Liz and me carry on a lengthy discussion about the incomprehensible way she was being treated by the man she was dating. This

131

guy would show up to get her more than an hour late. He would call her and cancel right before they were supposed to go out somewhere. And sometimes he would stand her up altogether.

They really had a good time, and a very romantic time, when they were with each other, however. So she was doing her best to try and figure out how to make their relationship healthier and less hurtful for her.

She turned to Charlie and said, "I just don't understand why he does this to me."

"He has bad manners," Charlie replied.

"Okay, I guess that's so," Liz agreed. "But why? Why does he behave this way? Is he playing hard to get? Is he honestly just that scatterbrained? Is he seeing someone else? You're a man, you tell me."

"Who knows why? It doesn't matter why," said Charlie. "The fact is he has bad manners. Is that okay with you, or not?"

End of topic. Much as both Liz and I enjoy jawboning on relationship issues, we had to agree that Charlie had tidily summed up the situation. He'd summed it up well enough that there was no further need for analysis. At least not on Liz's part. The only helpful analysis might come at the point where Mr. Bad Manners seeks help from a therapist as to why he is never capable of having anything but short-term relationships.

So I can't say that women are fundamentally better at relationships than men are. Men and women are just different. Maybe that
shouldn't be surprising. Maybe what's surprising is that the two
genders get along as well as they do. Either way, for me the differ-
ences underline the importance of having both men friends and
women friends. Of having a husband and also a bunch of girlfriends, both intimate in their own irreplaceable way.

One thing that's really great about my husband Michael is that
he has a good memory. Not about everything, of course. Only I, for
example, have the ability to quote exact transcripts of our conversations and arguments.

But he remembers the big stuff. He remembers that when we
met, one of the things he liked about me was that I had several
friends whom I loved and frequently devoted my time to. He knew
it didn't make sense, even if he were so inclined, to marry me with
the intention of changing that about me or taking over complete
control of my calendar.

I had room for a husband in my life, but I didn't have a huge
gaping hole. And even if I'd had a huge gaping hole, I know I
couldn't expect a mere mortal of a man to fill it.

chapter 7

Supermom I'm not

~7~

Soon after I had my first baby, an elderly neighbor came over with a warm loaf of zucchini bread, to treat me and to get her first look at new little Belle. I answered the door in my bathrobe and slippers, babe in arms.

"Oh, I'm sorry," said this lovely lady, hair done up to a tee. "I guess I'm coming over a little early. You haven't even had time to get dressed yet!"

Well, hello, of course I hadn't had time to get dressed—I'd only had four days. It had been six days since I'd had the baby and four since I'd come home from the hospital, but everyone knows you can't get dressed within the space of four days if you're taking care of a brand new baby girl. Getting clothes on would have required approximately eleven minutes, counting a superfast shower, and I didn't feel that I'd had nearly that much time to myself. Not nearly. Not since Belle came trundling down the old canal.

I did find time to thank my neighbor for the zucchini bread and scarf it down, but I think it was day eight before I managed to wash my hair, get dressed in real clothes, and actually put earrings on.

Looking back, I realize I was a bit unbalanced. But taking care of my precious and fragile infant at the beginning seemed like it required my concentrated attention at every waking moment. Every sleeping moment too. So I was never really sleeping soundly, not the way I'd slept the previous thirty-eight years. I'd wake up if Belle took a breath with a booger in her nostril. I could hear the soft clatter of a stuffy nose through the thin wool of my sleep from ten yards. And I must say it's impossible to get into a nice deep sleep when you're listening for mucus—especially if you're under the impression that mucus is deadly.

My husband didn't share my new-parent paranoia, though, happily for him. He slept like a log, which as any new mom can corroborate is what people mean when they use the phrase "slept like a baby." My little babies never slept like logs. Sleep for Belle and for Joe during the first several weeks of their lives seemed to have as much to do with waking up as it had to do with sleeping. But Michael was in the log category. He sawed logs while sleeping like one. Perhaps it was because he was so very well-rested that he was inclined to be so helpful with the baby when he arose.

"Do you want me to change Belle's diaper for you?" he inquired one morning upon gently rolling himself out of a nice long night of pleasant dreaming. This made me want to stuff him down the Diaper Genie and give it a good hard twist.

"For me?" I replied. "You're asking if I want you to change her diaper *for me?*"

Like I said, I know I was off-kilter. I'd sustained a near-perpendicular drop in hormone levels, in addition to suffering from the scabby nipples of a first-time nurser. But none of that is what caused my incredulity. I was alarmed by what I believed Michael was communicating to me, probably without meaning to, by phrasing that question as though he'd be extending me his largess by changing Belle's diaper.

What I seemed to be hearing was that my husband of one year considered child rearing to be the woman's and only the woman's job. Believe me, I realize we're living in a sexist society, but I was stunned. This little lump of information had never worked itself into our conversations during the courtship phase.

Michael's a considerate person, of course, and he was willing to help me with my job, but it wasn't his job. I was floored by his Neanderthal point of view and he was every bit as floored by my complete ingratitude.

He realized it was better for me not to be irritated, though, and things changed. Later he would not ask if I wanted him to do me the favor of changing our daughter's diaper. He would simply declare, "I changed Belle's diaper."

My reaction to that? I was irritated.

But in case you've now decided you're on my husband's side rather than mine, let me explain. Michael would say "I changed Belle's diaper" in exactly the same way he might say "I overhauled the transmission in your car." As in, "There, *that's* done." He didn't seem to grasp the fact that her diaper would need to be changed more than 4,000 times in the next three years. So while it might be a good thing that he went ahead and changed her diaper, I didn't appreciate his coming in and announcing it in a manner that was meant to make him look good for the next couple of weeks.

Plus, what if I did that to him? I think it would sound pretty fishy if I reported back to him hourly, "I changed Belle's diaper, and I washed, dried, and folded her jammies, and I ran her bottles through the dishwasher, and I nursed her for, oh, about twenty minutes, and I gave her a bath, which was fun although it did get her wet, but not to worry because I dried her."

Michael would've wondered why I had to update him on all of that, and I'm sure it would also have made him feel like he couldn't win.

Let's be honest about that, though—he couldn't win! We were both beginning to realize that I was always going to win in this category, because I was always going to do more than he did when it came to our kids. I resigned myself to that finally, and accepted the fact that the responsibility of taking care of our children was going to fall more on my shoulders than on his, especially when the kids were little. But I've only acquiesced to this because I think we've divided up the total number of jobs, inside and outside the house, pretty evenly. Not because I really believe that child rearing by its very nature should always be the woman's job.

I think it's easy for men to let themselves off the hook with certain things by telling their wives, "But dear, you're so much better at it." It's easy for them to say that about stuff like housekeeping, cooking meals, and raising children. I'm sure they think it's true. And maybe it's also tempting for us women to buy into that belief, staking out this territory as though we'd lose our status in the world if we didn't continually assert our congenital superiority to men in domestic skills.

"No, Michael, don't dust the end tables—your wrists can't swivel like mine and if you miss the corners I'll just have to do it over!"

"Please! Let me butter that toast, you're muscling it to death!"

"And for godsake, that's not how you put a T-shirt on a toddler—do you want his ears to stay like that?!"

I'm afraid that sounds a little like some of the stuff I've said, but actually I don't think I buy it. I don't really believe that we women can just naturally do all that stuff better than men. Yes, men and women are inherently different. But men have traditionally had jobs as janitors, so I know they're not incapable of house cleaning. Men have traditionally had jobs as chefs, so I know they're not incapable of cooking food. And I know from being married to my own husband that men can also be kind, playful, and nurturing parents, even to very small children.

Michael might have been a little overwhelmed, just as I was, by how much responsibility a new baby really involved at the beginning. But in my opinion he's turned out to be a wonderful father. Our parenting partnership has also edged closer to an even split in the seven years since we had Belle, social norms notwithstanding. Belle was only twenty months old when Joe came along, and things were markedly different when we brought Joe home from the hospital than they had been with Belle.

Most important, I was different. I had some confidence by then that Joe would survive if I left him in his crib to nap while I took a shower and got dressed. I knew he probably wouldn't die of boogers, anyway.

But Michael was different too. The minute I became a mom I became a light sleeper, and I'm afraid I'll probably never change back. But my husband didn't exactly slumber away Joe's infancy the same way he had with Belle. After my three-month maternity leave was over and I had to report back to my job, I got Michael to agree that it was only fair for us to take the nighttime feeding detail on alternate nights.

So my husband and I took turns getting up with Joe until he got to where he was sleeping through the night, at about four-and-a-half-months of age. Yes, I always woke right up when Joe cried, even on my nights off, and sometimes Michael didn't, but I wasn't opposed to striking him in the calf with my heel when necessary to remind him of his duty. I had to be at work in the morning just like he did.

But I was amazed that he was the only father we knew of who did this. He is still one of the few men I know who can actually appreciate, firsthand, what it is like to have your sleep interrupted again and again for more than a month straight, and then go in and try to be brilliant at work. He is still one of the few men I know who has shown up to a morning meeting with trails of spit-up on the back of his shirt.

I also think Michael's realized during the seven years since we had our first baby that he has more capabilities as a father than he might have assumed. He can be just as loving and nurturing as a woman can be, because he chooses to be. And he's been richly compensated too. My husband enjoys the same intimacy and warmth with our two children that I so treasure for my own self.

But the fact that I expect my husband to do a large share of the work is certainly not the only thing that makes me a slacker wife when it comes to bringing up baby. I think raising kids doesn't need to be as difficult as our generation seems to be making it, and I noticed right away that I was willing to do less than so many other moms around me.

Partly because I believe my kids are capable of doing quite a bit for themselves. I've observed that most parents of young children, including Michael and me, are constantly marveling at how brilliant their little offspring are. We're surprised again and again at our children's ability to remember and process things that we assumed had gone over their heads. We're amused and daz-zled by their ability to come up with their own ideas and unique takes on things, and throw modesty to the wind when recounting these incidents to others. They have functioning brains which are separate from ours—it's completely miracu-lous! And yet if the kid goes to make their own sandwich, many parents will jump up and say, "Here, let me do that for you."

I do appreciate how wonderful it is to be needed by a small child, though. In fact I hope that someday I'll still be needed by two of them when they're all grown up. But I know we'll all be in trouble if I'm still making their sandwiches for them.

I'm only exaggerating a little bit when I cite that as a danger. One of my pro-bono advertising clients is a turnabout program for delinquent girls, sort of a last-ditch effort to rehabilitate law-breakers and hopefully keep them out of real prison. I was joking with one of their counselors one day about how Belle and Joe think they're chefs because they can make their own baloney sandwiches, and she said, "Don't laugh. Making their own sand-wich is exactly the kind of thing the girls in our program don't know how to do. They've never experienced the joy and pride of solving even that kind of simple problem for themselves and learning that practical skill."

"In fact," she went on, "most of the girls in the program come from what you'd call 'privileged' homes. They've been given every advantage, but no responsibility. And they have zero self-esteem."

Yikes. After I heard that, I wondered if I should be having Belle and Joe prepare meals for the whole family, not just themselves.

I do want to be there for my children, though, and of course I want to help them. It's my job as a parent. But my client in the wayward girls program had seen for herself many times that we can sometimes end up hurting our kids by helping them too much. As radio commentator Paul Harvey said in an e-mail that was passed along to me, "We tried so hard to make things better for our kids that we made them worse."

"For my grandchildren," he wrote, "I'd like better. I hope they learn to make their own bed and mow the lawn and wash the car."

Now, I must admit that when I first read that I said to myself, "Not *my* car." Paul Harvey has never witnessed what Joe can do with a water hose, especially one that has a squirt nozzle on the end of it. It's a lot safer just to pay the ten bucks at Supersonic.

145

It is Belle and Joe's job to water the plants, but they usually bungle that too. Deaths among our philodendrons have been due both to drownings and to droughts. They also have to help with dinner dishes, but I've calculated that I could probably load and unload the dishwasher twice by the time they get one set of dinner plates scraped off and put in there, at which time I'll probably have to make them go back and dig the spatula out of the garbage.

But although Belle and Joe don't do things perfectly, they love being given some free rein, and they like the idea that they're making a contribution. I realized that if I had to have every job done the way I'd do it myself, I wouldn't be able to give my kids any chores at all. It's more important just to do things, I guess, than it is to do things perfectly. For children or anyone else. And it's especially important to learn self-sufficiency, to know that you can do things for yourself and solve your own problems without your parents always jumping in to control the outcome.

I don't have to tell Joe that, though. I believe his four favorite words at the age of five are "I don't need help." He's not always right about that, but I love him for being so game. So even though I'm often itching to take over and zip his coat or make his bed or pour his milk, I try to get out of his way as much as I can stand to.

Admittedly, that sometimes means allowing him to stumble and fall, both literally and metaphorically. But I'm always amazed at how quickly he and Belle recover and how readily they catch on to things. I'm sure that's one reason I haven't bought in to all of the childproofing measures that are recommended to parents these days. It just doesn't feel like a reliable formula that children should not be taught about the world; that the world should instead be rearranged for them.

That might be all right in the very short run, but the world won't change for children in the long run. We might run and catch them a hundred times, but gravity will get them in the end.

Of course I want Belle and Joe to be safe. But most of the time it must be safer to teach even young children to watch out for themselves, to teach them about the dangers rather than try and eliminate the dangers altogether. I told a story in my first book, *Confessions of a Slacker Mom,* about remodeling our kids' bathroom. The plumber, with the best of intentions, had set the valve so that when you turned on the bathtub faucet, it was bare-ly warm. You could run a bath at full-blast hot and it would hardly be comfortable. I called him and asked him to come back and reset it so that there was at least a semblance of hot water.

He explained to me, though, that it was a safety measure that would keep my kids from burning themselves.

Really, it would? He'd eliminated the hot water in the kids' bathroom, but he hadn't turned it off in the master bathroom or in our kitchen. And how about the neighbors and the friends up the street? Should I send our plumber over to their houses to see if they'd be willing to live without hot water, too, so that my children would not have to risk getting burned?

I doubted it. But Belle and Joe, then at the ages of five and three years old, already understood how to avoid that anyway. I had taken a little time to teach them the difference between the hot valve and the cold, and why that was important, and they grasped it right away. It seemed like a more feasible plan to arm them with information and with judgment than to try and rid the world of either hot water or most other dangers.

Some dangers I don't think the world should be ridded of anyway. Germs, for instance. I've already admitted I'm not a fan of excessive cleanliness, but I'm actually very suspicious of antibacterial soaps. I know the manufacturers aren't worried about me, though. Their sales are going gangbusters without me. In fact, these products are so popular that it's hard to buy a soap marketed for children that's *not* antibacterial. And there are now not only soaps but laundry detergents, shampoos, toothpastes, body washes, dish detergents, and lots of household cleaning products that are also lethal weapons in our war against bacteria.

We're out to kill them all, the poor little organisms. And after they've done us so much good all these years. As our pediatrician told me when Belle was a baby, children must be exposed to germs during their early years in order to develop the antibodies they'll need to fight infection later in life. He said not to worry about sterility unless we were hanging around someone who had a serious contagious disease. And I read of one study that said kids who are not exposed to common bacteria, which are wiped out by antibacterial soap, may be more prone to developing both allergies and asthma.

Yet sales of this stuff are still strong, and I probably shouldn't be surprised that my personal boycott hasn't dampened the enthusiasm. I'm sure parents continue to buy these products because they're told by those who are marketing them that that is exactly what conscientious parents do. I saw one commercial that showed an exceptionally good mom going out to spray disin-fectant on the ball her kids were playing with in the yard.

That woman is a crackpot for sure, but I do have to give her something—at least her kids were out playing in the yard. She's

149

not quite as daft as the woman in the minivan commercials, the one who does nothing but drive her children all over hell and gone to participate in afterschool activities. You know, I don't remember ever seeing a dad in one of those commercials either. The burden of shuttling the kids from one enriching experience to another usually seems to fall on the wife, not the husband.

I know this sounds lazy to some, but I'm not willing to spend my day running back and forth across town to make sure that Belle and Joe keep up with all the other kids. Nor do I want my kids' childhood memories of me to be all about the back of my head as I drive them around in the car. I'm sure that all of the available activities, taken one at a time, might have their merits, but when you start adding them together you can quickly get to the point where you're taking away more than you're adding. If the mom and the children are always overloaded and stressed out, it seems a lot more like a disadvantage than an advantage.

Belle does take piano lessons, and so far she's quite the happy little plunker. She'd like to do gymnastics too, which is probably fine with me, depending on the schedule and location. I'm okay with a couple of activities. But two activities, each once a week, is plenty for us. Some people I know have two a day. Some people have two a day for each kid. Maybe that's okay for some—it depends on what's important to you. But once you go down that road it might be difficult to put things in reverse, because it's so much easier to add things to your schedule than it is to take things off.

It's not just my reluctance to drive myself insane by overloading our schedules, though. I also wonder, if I left my kids with no time or opportunity to think for themselves and solve their own problems, even in terms of coming up with something to do to entertain themselves, whether I would really be enriching them. It feels more like shortchanging them. And I wonder, if my daughter always had to leave home in order to qualify as doing something worthwhile, whether she would have the opportunity to develop strong relationships with her brother, her father, or me. I wonder, if my son was pushed to achieve from the time he was two, whether he might burn out at ten.

And I wonder if there is any evidence that success in life is so formulaic that we can program our kids to succeed just by enrolling them in enriching activities from the time they are small. How do we know it's not just as enriching, and just as likely to lead to success in life, for them to be mowing the lawn or washing the car?

Some friends of mine went touring around to look at colleges for their teenagers last year, and came back with an interesting story. They were speaking to the Vice-Provost at one of the most

151

prestigious private colleges in the South, and he told them that these days when their admissions department sees applications from high school students that look almost as though they've been professionally crafted, it's a turnoff. The students who will end up being the leaders and the creative thinkers of tomorrow, he said, are not the ones who've been following some prescribed formula for success all of their early years, going from one instructor or coach or tutor to another to be told what to do and how to do it.

When I heard that story, part of me said, "Yes! I knew it, I knew it." But part of me said, "That dang Vice-Provost, whatever that is. If he's changed the rules, he ought to get on national TV right now and make sure every parent knows it. We've been going overboard all this time because we thought we had to!"

If his remarks inspire you not to go overboard yourself, though, you'll open yourself up for being criticized as a lazy mom like myself. But I would not assume that Belle and Joe are worse off just because I might be better off. Do our interests never coincide? Is it not important for them to have happy parents?

I want our family to operate as a team, actually, which means the world can't revolve around just one of us, or just the kids. We all ought to be willing and able to compromise and do things that may not be our first choice but might be best for the other person. Yes, I want even my children to understand compromise and thoughtfulness. I want them to grow up being mindful of the needs and desires (and schedules) of others. And I definitely don't want to saddle them with the shock and bewilderment of learning only later in life that the world does not in fact revolve around them.

Unfortunately, though, motherhood still seems to be closely associated with martyrdom. If someone argues that a thing is good for the kids, then it doesn't matter if it is bad for the mom. Even better, probably.

And it's not easy to back off when every other parent around you seems to be operating at hyperspeed. It's not easy to be zigging while everyone else is zagging. In fact—not that I'm trying to avoid being called a slacker—I think it's actually more difficult for parents to slack off than it is to go overboard.

When our kids are little, we parents are so in love with them that we almost can't help but want to give them everything. By the time a kid is grown-up, it might be easier for us to look back and understand what the consequences were, for the children themselves, of having been raised that way. Maybe that's why so much of the parenting advice I really do appreciate has come from those who are grandparents.

By the time you're a grandparent, it's easier to see that twenty years of age is a little late for a kid to learn for the first time
how to think for himself and make up his own mind about what's
important to him. It's a little difficult to start learning at twenty
how to handle setbacks, how to be resilient and try again. And
the stakes are a little high at twenty if you're just finding out that
the world is dangerous, and that you're vulnerable, and that you'd
better take responsibility and watch out for yourself because
there's not always going to be someone there to do that for you.

But I understand fear. I understand the kind of fear you could
never feel just for yourself. The profoundly dark fear you didn't
know you could feel at all until the moment you become the
mother of a wrinkly, squally, precious baby. I remember back
when I feared that Belle would surely be done in by a stuffy nose.
I just don't want all my decisions as a mom to be driven by fear.

What helps me the most is that my husband, whom I so
respect and admire, is not so fearful. He shares my point of view
about doing less and allowing our children to do more.

It's true that Michael hardly ever knows what time Belle's
piano lesson is, what swimming suit still fits Joe, or whether or
not they're expected at a birthday party this coming weekend.
But he has the same optimistic faith in Belle and Joe that I do. So

I guess I don't mind too much when I'm the one who will probably have to go out and buy yet another birthday gift for yet
another five-year-old.

Although I do think it might be funny to ask my husband if
he wants me to do it *for him.*

chapter 8

---

*I knew there was something
I forgot to do today!*

—8—

When I was first thinking about writing *Confessions of a Slacker Wife,* I told my friend Katherine about it to find out what she thought of the idea. The title alone caused her eyebrows to jump up to the middle of her forehead.

"Slacker wife, huh?" she repeated. "That's brave. Because you know you're going to have to talk about sex."

That had certainly occurred to me, but I figured my grandparents were going to read this book, so I'd ruled it out.

"Oh, no," I explained, "I'm not going to be talking about sex. This book's going to be more about stuff like chores."

"Same diff'."

Now, why Katherine can't articulate herself more succinctly, why she insists on beating around the bush like that, I don't know. But I did know she was probably right when she said I'd have to write about sex if I was going to write about life as a wife. I could picture myself with an X-acto knife, too, surgically removing the chapter in its entirety before giving the book to my grandparents, mumbling something about discount binding jobs.

But I also felt I should thank Katherine, because part of me realized that she'd just about written half the chapter for me. That would have made it a pretty short chapter, and a cynical one, but I had to admit that she'd said just about as much as I've ever heard anyone else say about the whole sorry situation, in just two words. She's a busy wife and mom just like I am, and at some point sex had become just one more item on her to-do list, and I felt pretty much the same way she did.

There's probably nothing more effective than putting sex on a to-do list if you want to take all the fun out of it:

MONDAY

- Dogs to groomer
- Call accountant
- Groceries for lunches
- Get Joe's glasses repaired
- Return Belle's shoes
- Pay utility bills
- Sex

It's hard for me to believe that Michael and I could ever get to the point where sex actually had to be scheduled, because we are genuinely attracted to each other. But I don't think we're the only couple who's verged on that. From what I hear at Book Club, that's about the way it is in lots of busy married lives. And even worse, in my marriage as in the marriages of many of my girl-friends, it's easy to let sexual intimacy become such a low priority that it doesn't make it onto the schedule at all.

For one thing, unlike a lot of the other stuff I need to get done, such as filing the tax return, making lunches for school, or paying bills, sex has no deadline. On any given day, we can always do it tomorrow. And on most days, tomorrow sounds preferable because today, I'm really just too tired.

I'm sure I've probably spent enough time in previous chapters talking about all the reasons why I might be tired. I've talked enough about child rearing and laundry and housecleaning and entertaining and social schedules and then there's my job . . . so I probably don't need to go on any longer establishing what it is that makes a wife like myself just a little fatigued when she falls into bed at the end of her day.

My husband might be tired too, but that's different.

Why? His sex drive just doesn't get derailed by four loads of laundry the way mine does. And that's not only because he hardly ever does laundry. His sex drive doesn't tend to get derailed if he goes out and chops firewood either.

I used to be more like him, as I recall; I used to be someone whose sex drive was pretty resilient. But I feel like my body has almost been reprogrammed as I've gotten older. It's communicating to me differently now. When Michael and I were first married, my body said to me, "Reproduce! Reproduce! It's just what you were made to do!"

But it doesn't say that now. Now it says, "Stop reproducing! Stop! You've got your hands full with just the two offspring, and your eggs are old!"

It's obvious to me that this is not my fault. I'm receiving these signals from somewhere deep in my system, perhaps the pituitary gland. At least I think I remember some visuals associated with that from a seventh grade sex education film—a stream of tiny ping pong balls issuing from a little globular mass under my brain, advancing with their instructions, ping, ping, ping, directly down to my reproductive organs.

The idea of those ping pong balls pelting along on autopilot made me feel a bit helpless when I was twelve, and it does now. It also seems unfair, because from what I can tell my husband's glands don't send the same signals to him that mine send to me.

I know for sure his body's not telling him that his eggs are old, and his sperm probably aren't even worried about how old they are, and he's got a zillion of them anyway. I don't suppose his body is telling him he's already got his hands full either. It's probably just saying, "Go for it, dude—in fact, do it every chance you get, because you've got to spread your seed throughout the land before some other dude does." Of course our marriage bed doesn't exactly amount to "throughout the land," but I think Michael's glands, if they were completely in charge of his mind, would absolutely have him going throughout this land and then on to the next.

Besides, a man Michael's age, or any age, assumes no health risk if a baby is conceived, so why not? My body might be counseling me not to get pregnant, but his is saying, "Pregnancy? Dude, that's not our problem." (You might notice that Michael's glands have a juvenile way of speaking compared to mine, but I admit that this is pure conjecture on my part.)

I've had little talks with my body, explaining that I am taking birth control measures, but it doesn't heed me. It's still stuck in an evolutionary rut that was established long before the Pill was invented.

So it feels like I'm in a tug of war with myself sometimes. I want to have sex in our marriage, but I'm not only busy and tired, I also feel like I'm going against my own hormonal inclinations.

And thus it's easy to let sex descend further and further on my list of priorities. At which point my husband starts to feel neglected, and sometimes resentful.

And that, of course, is just more good news. Now I can feel guilty on top of everything else, and that backfires thoroughly every time. Guilt makes sex very much less attractive, not more. Guilt as a sexual turn-on simply doesn't work well for me.

I'm turned off, frankly, by the idea that I should feel guilty about sex or the lack thereof because it's something that I owe to my husband. What do I owe him for? That might sound like a stupid question to some people, because the phrase "wifely duty" is well established as a nice-nellyism for sex. But I can't seem to think what debt I need to be paying off by having sex with my husband.

I know that women used to feel a sense of indebtedness. Her "wifely duty" used to be the least a wife could do to pay her husband back, what with all the time he spent slaving away at his job in order to keep a roof over her head and aprons on her back. But that was back when staying at home running the household and taking care of the children wasn't attributed the value it really deserved. A stay-at-home wife, back when her contribution wasn't deemed equal to her husband's, was undoubtedly in a subordinate position. The husband did indeed think she owed him, and she probably agreed.

But I think—I hope—that in today's society most people have a lot higher estimation of the woman who is a stay-at-home mom. They know the very term "stay-at-home" is a laughable misnomer. And they know she's doing a job which is demanding and difficult. They also acknowledge that her willingness to do it is probably a key reason why the husband can pursue his own career in the first place. So it's not surprising if today's wife tends to resist any suggestion that she ought to give her husband sex just because he shows up with some pay stubs.

And in some households, the husband doesn't have any pay stubs anyway. In even more households, he might have them, but so does his wife. Either way, whether one spouse or both of them are working at a job outside their home, the idea of sex as repayment seems egregiously outdated. And even if it weren't outdated, you must admit that it's vulgar beyond words.

Speaking of vulgar and outdated (not outdated enough to be out of use, though), here's a saying about men, women, and sex that I've always found completely appalling. "Why would he buy the cow," the adage goes, "when he's getting the milk for free?"

Of course, you don't have to speak hillbilly to know that the
phrase "buy the cow" translates directly to "marry the woman."

That right there is enough to make me triple perturbed. But I
can't resist breaking it down further. Let's talk about the word
"buy" in this context. When I was single, I do remember thinking
of myself as available, but not available for purchase. I was available for a mutually satisfying partnership based on commitment
and on love, one in which neither person owned or took posses-
sion of the other. And what about the word "cow" here, as a
reference to women? That must be one of the more regrettable
metaphors, even among hillbilly proverbs.

The individual word choices don't irk me as much as what
that backwoods saying in its entirety is meant to convey, though.
I don't like the idea—and I can't imagine what woman or man
would like the idea—of sex being positioned as something the
woman may give to the man or may withhold from the man,
depending on whether or not he's willing to "buy the cow," i.e.,
marry her, i.e., support her. It's just another installment in the sex-
as-repayment way of thinking, and it's also suggesting that the
only reason he *would* support her is if she gave him sex.

I might not have any argument with this idea if it worked
both ways. But like so many other sexual standards, it doesn't. In

any situation where a man is "getting the milk for free," i.e., getting sex without having to pay for it, the woman involved is obviously getting sex too. Yet no one says she is "getting the milk for free." Just the opposite, because she is the *vendor*, not the *customer*. She's not *getting* sex, she's *giving away* sex! In other words, she's not getting compensated, the little floozy. Ironic, I think, that we're supposed to think more highly of her if she refuses to do it unless she does get compensated, because I think the expression for the woman who does that is "working girl."

I must admit I like the expression "working girl" better than "cow," but that doesn't mean I want to be a working girl in my marriage. I never made a bargain with my husband that had him buying groceries and me servicing him. Tit for taters. I'm buying quite a few taters with my own paycheck, anyway.

So perhaps he's here to service me, then. After all, I did marry him and I also do my part to support our family, so I've bought the cow. That probably wouldn't work, though. Because I believe that Michael, over the long run, would be as turned off by the idea of obligatory sex as I am.

Wait a minute, though, here's what he could do. He could just trot over to the grocery store to pick up a handful of women's magazines, because I've noticed that women's magazines frequently have articles that provide foolproof little gimmicks which allow us women to get past our own sexual reluctances and hang-ups. So who knows, maybe those tricks and techniques would work just as well for Michael.

Sexy lingerie does the job, they say, and I would be very intrigued to see my husband step out of the bathroom in a black mesh corset. Scented candles, body oils, dirty language—these things also purportedly work like magic. And according to one article I read, so does open and frank discussion about specific body parts and sexual techniques, even during sex itself.

Yuck, though. I'm not too sure my husband would get excit-ed about employing any of those methods. And I know I can't pretend I want to engage in them myself. I'm not too sure that any of that stuff by itself really works anyway. Maybe sometimes it does, but a lot of times I think women's magazines are just dish-ing out these supposedly new (though so often repetitive) formulas for sex and romance because that's what they think we want to hear.

I say that partly because of my own experience with the edi-torial policies of women's magazines. For instance, one time I was asked to write an article for a women's magazine in which I was to report to its readers the results of a little experiment the magazine asked my husband and me to conduct. The experiment they assigned to us had to do with PDA, or public displays of affection. Over the course of one week, my husband and I were to engage in PDA at every opportunity and find out if it served to spice up our sex life at home.

So we did the experiment, and I turned in the article. A few weeks later, I got an e-mail back from the editor I'd been work-ing with.

"The writing is great and very funny," she wrote. "I laughed out loud at least three times reading it. But I think my chief was hoping for a more positive outcome—that it would have spurred more romance behind the scenes. I actually found the way it unfolded incredibly realistic, but I guess it's just not working for our chief."

You see, as I had recounted in my article, public displays of affection had not spurred more romance behind the scenes for Michael and me. And not because we hadn't really given it a go, because we had. We'd tried to make out at the movie, but it was difficult for me to kiss him while positioning my head so I could continue watching what was happening on the screen. I started rubbing Michael's thigh quite seductively one afternoon while one of our friends was being sworn in as a circuit court judge, but he actually said, "Stop it," which took the romance right out of it.

Michael took the lead himself one evening while we were standing in line for food at a wedding reception, but while I appreciated his efforts, I also wished he hadn't been rubbing circles on my bottom like a drunken clod. It caused my dress to hike up higher than my slip and I was sure the people behind us in the buffet line could see that.

So apparently, even though our results were "incredibly realistic," the experiment was a bust as far as the magazine was concerned. I was really disappointed by that assessment. Partly because my article wouldn't be running and I wouldn't be getting the fee I felt I'd earned, but partly because I didn't consider the experiment to be a bust at all, myself.

I actually thought we'd had a "positive outcome" because of what it had revealed about each of us. I was glad to have learned something about both myself and my husband, something about how we'd changed in the past twenty years. Both Michael and I were intrigued to discover how embarrassed we felt to be seen groping each other in public. We really didn't feel comfortable going much further than a peck on the cheek if other people could see us, and it was interesting to find that out. We'd turned into fuddy-duddies, that was the fact, and we were willing to admit it in a national magazine.

But I suppose magazines like to plan ahead, and the editor-in-chief had already been planning on different results. He or she didn't think that what had really resulted from our trumped-up experiment would be of interest to their subscribers, even if it did give them something to laugh at.

I hope the editor was wrong about that, though. Among the national women's magazines I'm familiar with, the one I'm talking about is one of the more literary and nonsuperficial. This magazine almost never has feature articles with their expert analysis of which mascara will truly stay on your eyelashes longer, and I would bet that their readers really do prefer reality to fantasy.

But I'm not a magazine editor, and I don't have to sit at the conference table and explain myself to the publisher. Or to the advertisers, many of whom are probably selling mascara. And it's probably a good thing I'm not a magazine editor too. Because while I might not think women's magazines have much more than pat answers about keeping sex alive in a marriage, I myself have hardly any answers at all.

I do have a few ideas for sarcastic rejoinders. One time my husband said, "I don't know what turns you on any more." And I said, "You turn me on, dear, vacuuming." He didn't think that was too funny as I recall, but I thought it was a clever way of communicating to him that a little more help with the house-hold chores would put him in good stead, and the truth is, it would.

But sarcastic rejoinders probably aren't what's needed for most husbands. Or most wives. Sarcastic rejoinders probably wouldn't even work as well as your average mesh corset. And even if Michael did vacuum the living room, even if he dusted the furniture and scrubbed out the toilet bowls, I'm not sure it would be a quick fix for our sex life.

I don't mean to sound like I have anything against quick fixes, by the way. Not if they really fix things, and why not fix things quickly rather than slowly? But PDA is not the only quick fix we've tried that didn't really fix things. In fact, although I am aware that the following statement will probably disqualify me from ever running for political office, let me just go ahead and divulge that I have purchased sex toys.

I decided it would be an extraordinary gesture on my part, above and beyond the call of my wifely duty, for one of Michael's recent birthdays. The only reason I was willing to set foot in the only local store I know of that sells this type of thing, The Blue Boutique, was that two of my friends volunteered to escort me. There is no way I would ever have appeared in this establishment by myself, and I was very surprised that my respectable girl-friends had had the audacity to shop in the place by themselves.

I'm the type of person who wonders what the checkout clerk is thinking if I buy extra-strength deodorant, so I would never have the guts to face the cashiers in The Blue Boutique without being part of a group. It seems that when you're all by yourself, any shopping trip assumes an air of serious intent, and I have no desire to be seen perusing products in The Blue Boutique with an air of serious intent. But if you go with two girlfriends, it changes the tenor entirely. The three of us could laugh and joke in a way that would undoubtedly indicate we were there for the sole purpose of obtaining gag gifts for some tacky bachelorette party.

Being with experienced friends did more than provide me with that kind of an iffy alibi, though. They also—in normal speaking voices which were audible throughout the store—dispensed consumer product information which was evidently critical.

"Don't buy this one. Mine actually broke, and they wouldn't exchange it."

"Oh, God—I remember when my husband thought this thing would be a good idea. What does he think I am, a hippo?"

"This one I would give five stars if it weren't about as loud as a lawnmower."

Anyway, after thirty of the most gripping minutes of my life, I walked out of there with the item that both friends agreed would be a solid purchase and a quality item which I would not regret owning.

And I also purchased a black mesh corset, if you've been wondering why I've seemed so knowledgeable about them.

The evening of my husband's birthday, we had a lovely dinner in a romantic restaurant and finished a bottle of wine. When we got home, Michael slipped into bed and picked up the TV remote. Meanwhile, I hoped he wouldn't notice that I varied my own routine by changing clothes in the bathroom.

A few minutes later, I emerged from the bathroom in my droopy flannel bathrobe and sauntered up to Michael's side of the bed with what I hoped was a very wicked look on my face. He stopped watching *Dateline* and stared at me expectantly, and then I threw open my robe with a flourish, unveiling myself in the black mesh corset, brandishing the Emperor's Wand in my right hand—certain that the whole thing would absolutely electrify him.

"Pfff—HA!"

That was my husband's spontaneous response, which struck me as artless in the extreme. But I realized I couldn't be too upset about it. His loud guffaw was probably no more artless than my heavy-handed attempts to quite suddenly be over-the-top sexy. The only thing to do was to gather up my robe and fall on the bed, laughing helplessly at my own thorough embarrassment.

Laughter really is an aphrodisiac for Michael and for me, so my plans for his birthday night didn't ultimately end in failure. But we laugh at the same things because we honestly do see eye-to-eye as to what's funny, and we've gotten to be even more that way over the years of our marriage. So I can't even recommend laughter as a quick fix, because I don't think you can force it any more than you can force a sudden transformation of yourself from fairly traditional wife to sizzling dominatrix.

From what I read and from what I see on television, the sexless marriage is one of the hottest topics on talk shows and in magazines, and a lot of people smarter than myself are tackling the problem. So that's good, because as I said I don't have any tricks up my sleeve. That's not to say my purchase from The Blue Boutique doesn't "work," because if you want to have sex with yourself, then I must say that whoever is designing these devices has got it down to a science.

But I don't much want to have scientifically calibrated sex with myself, not when I'm married to a warm and affectionate person like Michael Ferro. So my Blue Boutique item has generally remained at the bottom of my sock drawer inside a pair of knee-highs. I certainly can't donate it to the Salvation Army's small appliance department along with our duplicate coffee grinder. And I am too paranoid to put it out in our own garbage cans, because the automated pickup arm has been known on rare occasions to let things fall out of the container and onto the street, where the item then sits in plain sight in front of our curb until Michael or myself gets home in the evening.

I'm no expert, though, and I wouldn't want to say that sexual techniques and methods can't be learned, or even that battery-powered accessories are never beneficial. I know one woman who says that she just gets started, for instance, and the desire follows. If that can be categorized as a method, then it seems like one that's worthwhile.

But all I can tell you is the method that's worked for me. And I don't mean what's worked for hot-and-steamy sex by Saturday, I mean what's worked over a long period of time. That is, when I realized that it was the idea of obligatory sex that was so completely unappealing to me, I mentally let myself off the hook. I took sex out of the chores category, and out of the things-to-do-for-my husband category, once and for all. In fact I told myself that as far as that went, I didn't ever have to have sex again for the rest of my life if I didn't want to.

Perhaps I should feel sheepish at how easily I can play psychological tricks on myself, but my immediate reaction to that idea was, Never again? Hold the phone—I believe I want it right this minute.

Once I stopped thinking of sex as a debt I owed, and a debt for which I was always in arrears, something interesting happened. Sex became a higher priority in my life. I started to focus on what I wanted rather than just on what I assumed somebody else wanted. And at the risk of sounding like I'm writing for a women's magazine, I must say that it's worked like magic, because by changing my perspective, it changed my attitude. Now when I get into bed, I am not asking myself, Will he or won't he make advances? I'm asking, Will I or won't I?

When I think about it that way, I'm truly surprised at how often the answer is, Yes, I will. And don't think any little ping pong balls are going to get in my way.

chapter 9

Trivial pursuits

-9-

My mother told me a story one time about driving my grandparents—who've now been married more than seventy years—from Jackson, Wyoming, to their winter home in a retirement community outside of Phoenix. It occurred to her about halfway through the fifteen-hour drive, taken over the course of two days, that there was something quite remarkable about it . . . something other than the 90-degree increase in ambient air temperature.

What so impressed her, she told me some time after the trip, was that rather than riding along silently like most people, her parents talked to each other (and to her, but mostly to each other) for the entire journey. They talked a little about what they'd eaten for breakfast, who'd been mowing their lawn, what the weather was doing. Mundane matters. But they spent a good part of the time talking about politics and global affairs. And they also talked about ideas—about computers, the cattle business, the geologic features they were passing on the side of the highway.

It seemed so wonderful and so out of the ordinary that after all those decades, these two people were still each other's most interesting companion. As well as each of them knew the other person, there were still new conversations to have, and so many of them were conversations about things with real substance.

I wasn't necessarily looking for a husband at the time my mom told me that story, but I remember that it prompted me to make the following mental note to myself: Make sure not to marry a dimwitted bore. And then after a few moments of thinking about it, to make the following additional mental note to myself: Make sure not to be a dimwitted bore.

I know I'm boring some of the time. And my husband isn't just spellbinding every moment himself.

But when we met, one thing that drew us steadily toward each other was that our interests and opinions on so many meaningful topics tended to coincide. I remember when we were dating that we'd stay up late at night and talk about all kinds of consequential things: religion, politics, finances, art. We discovered that as far as religion went, both of us are basically deists; we believe in God as a creator and prime mover, but don't believe in the kind of God that would meddle in the affairs of human beings, causing one country to be invaded or one college football

team to defeat another. On politics: We're both fiscally conserva-
tive, yet shockingly liberal on social issues, and can't identify
closely with either major party. On finances: Both of us feel more
confident investing money in some old building that needs to be
fixed up than in the stock market. On art: We listened to ourselves spout baseless hypotheses for a while and then agreed that
neither of us knows a thing about it.

Now that we've been married for eight years, however, we
don't have many late-night conversations about God, or art. We
have late-night conversations about baloney. Yes, baloney,
because it turns out that tomorrow is the one day of the week
that our son, Joe, will be in school all day, so he'll be needing a
sandwich to pack in his lunch box, and we are out of baloney.
Can't he just have a peanut butter sandwich? No, the school is
concerned with nut allergies. Can't he just have a tuna fish sandwich? No, he won't eat tuna. There's nothing to do but
rock-paper-scissors for the trip to the store.

You can see how much we've advanced and developed as a
couple.

I'm sure that happens to everyone, though, and I don't really
mind that we have late-night conversations about lunchmeat. But
I also remember how exhilarating it was to have our minds mesh

on more intellectual matters back when we were getting to know each other. Those conversations, more than any midnight make-out sessions on the sofa, were what bonded us to each other and ultimately led to our marriage.

Not only do I not want to lose that compelling intellectual connection that we started out with, but I also don't want to end up with nothing to talk to each other about once the kids are out of the house. That's why I so admire my grandparents' marriage. Their "kids" have been out of the house more than fifty years, and evidently they're still not bored with each other. I think they're the exception, though, because so often I've looked around at couples in restaurants or on airplanes and noticed that many of them don't actively converse with each other, and in some cases never even seem to look directly at each other. I don't think it's unusual to see couples at Sunday brunch reading their own separate newspapers.

I'm not saying I want to jabber with my husband every minute just because we happen to be in the same room. I've already said I'm comfortable with the idea of twin beds, so I'm okay with a little detachment. And I'm definitely comfortable with silence in a relationship from time to time. But I suppose that silence could also become quite persistent, a separation rather than a shared peace, so that eventually you could get to the point where you wouldn't have much more than "Think it'll rain?" and "It certainly could" to offer each other in the way of conversation.

Neither Michael nor I want to see our marriage go down that rat hole. On that we agree. But the danger of having nothing interesting to say, of lapsing into the trivial, is a little bit greater, I believe, for me than it is for him. Why? Because lunchmeat-level affairs tend to be foisted onto women far more often than they're foisted onto men. Especially by the media. Especially by the women's media.

There was the *Newsweek/Cosmopolitan* incident, for example.

This incident occurred several years after I heard the story about the drive to Arizona from my mother. By then she had died, and I was newly married to Michael. We had several minutes in which to relax before boarding our flight for our honeymoon, so as I sat in the waiting area at the gate, Michael went over to the concourse newsstand to pick up some last-minute items.

He came back with two packs of chewing gum and two magazines, *Newsweek* and *Cosmopolitan*. Goodness, what a considerate person my husband of fourteen hours was; he'd been thinking not just about himself but about me too.

"So," I asked him after he got settled back into his seat, "have you always been a *Cosmo* reader?"

"What? The *Cosmo* is for you, dumbhead."

"But dumbhead," I responded, "we can't talk about lip shimmers on the way to Arizona."

Of course, I think it's amusing to make incomprehensible remarks and I was tempted to just leave that one lying there. But I wanted to start our marriage off on a positive note, and perhaps with a little piece of instruction for my dumbhead new husband. Why not?

So I told Michael the little story that my mother had told me about driving my grandparents to Arizona. I told him I thought it was fairly crucial that we remain in the same league intellectually, assuming he could keep up. I told him I hoped that we'd always have the ability to converse about things for which we had mutual enthusiasm, and that I was frankly no more interested in reading *Cosmo* than he was.

Not because I was too old (oh all right, partly I was too old—I suppose their reader demographic must be in the eighteen-year-old range), but because from what I'd gathered, that particular magazine mostly covers matters that are of the very minutest significance. Matters which we would never discuss on a two-day car trip and which couldn't possibly have any lasting interest for him or for me. Matters which, if I allowed myself to focus on them, would very likely turn me into the greatest dimwitted bore.

I'm not sure if Michael completely agrees that fan-blown hair, child-size tank tops, and true gynecologist confessions are dull subjects. But he conceded that he too wanted us to have the kind of marriage my grandparents apparently have, and he didn't argue with me after that about whether or not I should be interested in *Cosmo*. I must say that I got the sense he was a little disappointed, nonetheless. I got the impression as he looked at the girl on the cover of the magazine and then looked back at me that he was thinking, "Are you absolutely sure you don't want to read this?"

I didn't, though, and I believe that's the last time Michael's ever purchased a women's magazine on my behalf. But I've been more cognizant, ever since the *Newsweek/Cosmopolitan* incident, of the way the media speaks to me and to other women, and how fundamentally different that is from the way they address our husbands.

Of course, I realized even back on our honeymoon that my role as a wife would involve plenty of tedium and plenty of conversations about baloney sandwich–type issues. I'm sure that

Michael and I aren't often going to have scintillating discussions about the lead article in *Scientific American*. But I know we're not going to have any scintillating discussions about the things I keep seeing in the women's media, either.

Not that I have zero interest in clothes, makeup, food, or housekeeping. But I've noticed that so many of the media and marketing messages directed to women these days are spending way too much time talking about those things and other things that are just as superficial—as though that's all we care about—and hardly ever about ideas. Hardly ever about business, global affairs, or the geologic features on the side of the highway.

Here's a smattering of the articles I found in women's magazines, just perusing their covers at the grocery store one day:

His Secret Pleasure Points

Choosing the Perfect Sofa

The Ten Biggest Beauty Mistakes

Whimsical Garden Whirligigs

Which Stars Are Racist

A Dozen Desserts They'll Die For

No More Bad Hair Days

Sex Sessions That Ended in the ER

Celebrity Cooking Gear

A Cat Puppet You Can Knit

New Fall Hair Trends

Celebs Who Admit to Surgery

Super Fat-Burning Foods

Our Editors' All-Time Top Makeup Picks

Sexed-Up Denim

Lose Weight in Your Face

I must concede that if someone wanted to knit me a cat puppet, I wouldn't mind it. And I must also concede that, in addition to the ones on the above list, I saw articles on breast cancer, home buying, and career management in many of the women's magazines I looked at. I don't know if these articles provided substantive, new information, but at least they were tackling substantive topics. Nonetheless, the preceding list is a fair sampling, I think, of the kinds of things we women are so often encouraged by the media to get ourselves wrapped up in.

The trivial nature of the subject matter in so many women's magazines and televisions shows is not what most disturbs me, however. What's even worse is the way they grind and grind and grind on these subjects in a way that's far out of proportion to their importance in our lives.

I wonder how many hundreds of magazine pages—both edi-
torial and advertising—have been devoted to the following topic,
for instance: eyeliner. Eyeliner, it seems, is a surprisingly intricate
matter. First of all, should it go on wet or dry? And should it be
applied with a pencil or brush? Should we draw it on just the
upper or on the lower lids too? With a hard line or a smudgy one?
Or should we just bet the farm and get our eyelids tattooed?

I would guess that millions of marketing and media dollars
have been invested in this deadly dull discussion over the years,
but it seems to me that these eyeliner issues could have been settled quickly and easily. It seems like they could have been put to
bed some time ago, with one or two 500-word articles, tops.

But media messages directed to women, particularly the ones
coming from marketers, continue to churn the developments in
eyeliner, along with so many other issues that are at or near that
level of hairsplitting triviality. Which handbag is most popular
with runway models. Which dish detergent dissolves grease
fastest in unscientific time trials. Which room freshener propels
its scent furthest out into the room. Which plastic bag has a clos-
ing mechanism that's more idiot-proof than the others. Which
salad dressing most reminds the paid actors of a country lifestyle.

As a slacker wife, I have no plans to keep abreast of ongoing
developments regarding any of the above.

The truth is, I don't really think these questions need to be settled. But I guess I don't have to worry about that, because I know they never will be settled. No handbag can be fashionable by the media's definition of "fashionable" for more than about five minutes. In fact it seems like the discussions surrounding these issues are actually designed that way: that not only are we talking about trivial things, we are talking about things which by design can never be resolved. We can revisit them over and over again and continue to expend both our mental energy and our money on the new "solution."

There's the Turkey Question, for instance. And no, I'm not talking about whether or not separatist Kurdish forces will threaten the stability of the government in Istanbul.

As I'm writing this, it's a few months away from Thanksgiving. And I've noticed that the checkout stands at the grocery store are already stocked with magazines that have roasted turkeys on the cover. Oh hurray, I think to myself, they're going to tackle the Turkey Question and explain to us wives how to cook a turkey. Never mind that American women have been cooking turkeys for Thanksgiving for literally hundreds of years. Because apparently the turkey pundits have finally determined how we can cook them exactly right, just in time for our

Thanksgiving dinners this very year, and now they're ready to give us the final word on it.

Turkeys are equivalent to handbags in this regard, though—it won't really be the final word. I'm sure that next year at about this time they'll have figured it out once again, in a way that causes millions of American women to buy the magazines and tune in to the cooking segments to find out the latest formula once again.

I just wonder if we're really moving forward on this issue, though. At least handbag styles really do undergo physical change. But do turkeys? One of the magazine articles I made note of promised "Your Most Golden Brown Turkey Ever." But I'm skeptical if the turkey I plan to cook this year—even if I give in and carry out their instructions to the letter—can really be that much more golden brown than the one I cooked last year. Will this year's turkey actually glow, I wonder, will it actually illuminate our dining room? And will it truly be so much more moist than my turkey has ever been before? Will it be so moist that it'll spray me with hot liquid when I start carving it? Or will it really be just about the same as it usually is, and pretty much the same as turkeys have been since about 1934?

I mention the year 1934 because that's the year my grandparents got married. I don't know if my grandmother cooked a turkey that year or not. But if she did, I know she didn't do it according to some novel methodology that made 1933's turkeys look substandard. What you basically did back at the time when she was a new bride was this: You put the raw turkey in a roasting pan and you put it in the oven, and you left it in there until it got re-e-a-al hot, even on its insides.

Does this sound familiar? Okay, perhaps you seasoned it and perhaps you basted it—but those kinds of tips you could get from your mother or your mother-in-law, so there was no real need for a new stack of magazines every year.

I envy my grandmother that. And I also envy her because the store she shopped in didn't have racks and racks of women's magazines anyway, and she didn't have a television to watch cooking shows with, and she wasn't made to feel, every time she went to do something as simple as cook a turkey, that she didn't know what she was doing, and that she wouldn't be able to do it satisfactorily without the very latest instructions. She simply learned how to cook a turkey, just the one time. And then I believe that she went ahead and moved on with her life.

I realize that poorly cooked turkeys have farther-reaching consequences than eyeliner gone awry. So the turkey discussion is not as trivial as some. But regardless of the significance of the issue, I can't see a reason to hash through it a million times. As much as I wish the media and the marketers would stop talking to us women about trivial things, I wish even more that they'd stop talking to us about the same things over and over. And I wish they'd stop creating the expectation that things are moving forward when we probably just keep going over the same tired and skimpy territory.

I also can't help but comment that there's much more ink devoted to the recipes and the decorations and the table settings of Thanksgiving than there is to the idea of Thanksgiving. And that seems like a considerable loss, because there was a worthwhile idea there, back when the first English settlers—people who were grateful to even be alive at that point—came up with it. I can appreciate how easy it is to forget the underlying idea of being thankful for the basic good things that we have, and I know how easy it is to forget to count our blessings and to remember how lucky we are if we have family, food, and home.

I know it's easy to forget those ideas because I usually do forget them. I know I need to be reminded of what Thanksgiving is all about as much as anybody else does. But I'm not sure I really have been reminded of it, by someone outside my own family, since I was in elementary school.

I suppose there's not much money in the mere idea of Thanksgiving, though. In other words, there probably aren't a lot of advertisers selling women's products that are associated with just being thankful. And if publishers can't sell ad pages on the subject, then they're probably not going to devote the editorial pages to it.

My guess is that's not a coincidence either, because I've noticed that there's not exactly a church-and-state separation between editorial content and advertising content when it comes to some women's publications. I've noticed that when a magazine's advertisers include lots of cosmetics companies, they're sure to have plenty of feature stories about the "new" makeup looks for spring (right on the heels of the ones for summer, fall, and winter) which will require you to throw out half the makeup you have and buy new.

Maybe that's why the "news" reported in so many women's magazines and television shows—news on things such as turkey cooking—doesn't often come off as something that's not already well known. Perhaps the feature stories for women truly are just as repetitive as they seem, because the advertisers who are footing the bill have got to keep their products moving off the grocery store shelves, in spite of the fact that so many products don't really have anything new to offer us, either. I saw one back cover ad for nail polish recently that went so far as to say their pink was actually a "reincarnation," they were so determined to make the idea of pink nail polish, centuries old, sound new.

I've observed that the messages to women are not only repetitive though, they're circuitous. It seems like almost any magazine that has a turkey or a chocolate cake or a big ol' pan of cheesy lasagna on the cover has at least one article about shedding pounds quickly and easily. I know very well how hungry it makes a person to go on a diet, and I also know how easy it is to talk about dieting when your stomach is full, so I guess that going around and around is not a psychologically unsound sales strategy for the magazines. I've noticed the same contradictions when it comes to relationships too, as they're covered by women's magazines. You can often find an article on How to Get a Man in the very same issue as What's Wrong With Your Man.

That might be a great convenience for us readers, but it would certainly help to explain why it feels like we really are going around in circles. With men, turkeys, eyeliner, and so many other subjects.

It would be one thing if I had nothing else to concern myself with. But I have a limited mental capacity, as well as a tight schedule. So while I worry about the fact that we women are constantly encouraged to focus on things that are in fact extremely trivial and superficial, I must say I worry even more about the opportunity cost for us if we do focus on them.

It's not just the question of what we'll have to talk to our husbands about when we're in our eighties, long after our children have families of their own. It's this question: How will we ever manage to compete with our male counterparts in business, and in politics, and in science, and in the arts, if we're fixating on the trivial? We women start off life with as much intelligence as men have, but we can hardly think of big ideas to change the world if we're having to expend our finite mental energy on whether or not our lips are shimmering, our toilets are sparkling, and what miniscule adjustments might have been made in the cooking of turkeys.

Of course, this frittering away of our female brainpower can certainly begin before we're married. But I can see how, if I combined a focus on picayune problems with my status as a wife, it might be even more perilous for me.

Being a wife, unfortunately, still carries with it the historical baggage of being in a subservient position. "Head of the household" was a phrase that was meant to connote the husband, of course, not the wife. People might avoid using that phrase these days, but I know that if I'm focused on recipes, dieting, makeup, hair styles, and decorating that I'm going to have an even more difficult time in this still-sexist society of remaining on equal footing with my husband.

We women might have made some strides as far as equality goes, but it seems like we're not making them in this particular area—in how the media speaks to us, in the superficial concerns they're reinforcing. In fact it seems like we're actually going backward in this regard. I'm inundated with these messages in a way that my mother and grandmother never were.

My daughter, Belle, so full of potential, is growing up female in this sexist and media-driven culture, and it worries me. I'll do my best to pass my skeptical outlook on to her, but I've noticed that her natural perspective is one of complete gullibility. She said to me one day, out of nowhere, "Mom, do you know what's really bad for you?"

I imagined she was on the topic of hot lava or poison apples. "What?" I asked.

"Tossing and turning."

"Really?"

"Yes." Adding, "I toss and turn all night on my old-fashioned spring mattress."

Another day she told me that we really needed to buy some of that Fledge.

"Fledge?"

"Yes, so we won't see fingerprints on the table."

Thank goodness Belle doesn't have access to our credit cards—she'd be the perfect consumer. She'll probably have her own credit cards someday, of course, so I'm doing my best to teach her to think for herself and to use her own judgment. I'm doing my best to raise Belle to someday be a slacker wife just like I am.

But I worry that if she reads magazines or watches TV, and she surely will, she'll grow up with the impression that the only things young women care about are the following: clothes, shoes, dieting, hair, makeup, and boys. And she's already gathered that what we more mature women care about are all of the above, plus ways of preparing food and methods of cleaning. Even when they're addressing such piffling problems as fingerprints on furniture.

Is this going to make her a better potential mate for someone? Honestly, I don't think it will.

I can see how it might make our husbands' dear male egos feel more secure if their wives were busy reading up on hair color, furniture polish, and drop-cookie recipes—and staying far afield of what men might think is their exclusive intellectual territory. Maybe it would make them feel more confident if their wives weren't worrying their pretty little heads with stuff like business or politics or philosophy—and wouldn't challenge their own thinking on those things.

But I don't think focusing on trivial issues would make us better wives, even if it would make our husbands feel smarter. In the long run, I think we'll have happier marriages if we're the intellectual equals of our spouses and share some common intellectual ground. At least we'll have things to talk about. It'll give us things to argue about too, but even arguing seems better than having nothing to say to each other. Especially if we're arguing about things that actually matter to us both.

Of course, every once in a while, my big brain is plumb worn-out, and I feel like the only thing that'll rejuvenate me is forty-five minutes as a full-blown intellectual slacker. At those times there's nothing better than reading up on fluff—the new way to cut your bangs, what celebrity marriage is in trouble, and yes, even ways of cooking a turkey—in a women's magazine as I polish my toenails in reincarnated pink. I'm sure we all need to be airheads, and to be able to laugh about it, from time to time. And I include men when I say "we all."

But most of the time, I'm simply not interested in so many of the things that society is telling me I'm supposed to care about as a wife.

Not only that, but I want my marriage to be a long and cap-tivating conversation, one that continues into our old age, one that can always strike out over unexplored terrain. I don't much want to talk about salad dressing, or room fresheners, or different ways of removing stains from carpet. And I can guarantee you that my husband doesn't want to discuss those things.

Although I do hope, if we ever end up driving to Arizona together, that he's not planning to talk about Monday night foot-ball, either.

chapter 10

—◆—

Slackers, unite

-10-

Let me just tell you what a detestable slacker my husband Michael is. He's a lazy bum, basically. A sluggard. A slouch.

Like so many other busy wives, stretched too thin, I tried for quite a while to come up with a way to convince my husband that he should take on more of the household duties. I launched into many an instructive monologue with him early in our marriage, explaining how unjust it was that although I was carrying half the husband's customary burden of being the breadwinner for our family, he was not carrying half the wife's customary burden in the domestic department.

Notwithstanding the fact that instructive monologues are my specialty, and notwithstanding the fact that I had an irreproach-able argument, this never did have the effect I intended for it to have with Michael.

"But you do all of that so much better than I do" was the gen-eral direction in which his responses skewed—a direction which might be considered crafty in the psychology department but falls completely apart in the substance department. He is perfectly capable of doing whatever he sets his mind to. My husband can detail a car and I'm sure he could do the same thing to a dining room if he chose to.

In fact I think I pointed that out to him one time, but nothing I've said has ever made much of a difference in my husband's slackerish ways. Michael evidently believes we can have people over without even picking up around the house first. He seems to think it's acceptable if the refrigerator drawers don't get cleaned out for two years. He doesn't care if the dinner napkins have been through the wash in recent history, and furthermore, is just as content to wipe off his face with a paper towel.

The man is something of a clodhopper, and apparently he won't be rehabilitated.

I think I beat my head against the wall for quite some time before I realized he was onto something.

The truth is, I just don't have it in me to be the quintessential wife, the model of domestic womanhood, any more than my husband has it in him. And what's even more truthful is that even if I did have the capacity, I can't seem to make it a priority. Because deep down I don't really think that's what's needed— not for the betterment of myself, of my community, or even of my own family. Deep down, I don't really think it would be worth the time or the effort that it would require. So I only manage to perform at that level in unpredictable, erratic, and short-lived spurts.

Every once in a great while I find it engrossing, for example, to sort through spinach quiche recipes on Epicurious.com to choose the one I think would be the ideal addition to an elaborate brunch I'm planning to prepare. Every once in a great while I get it in my head to give myself a beauty treatment and sit in a salt bath with a mud masque on my face, deliberately deluding myself into thinking it will make my skin look younger. Every once in a great while it even feels oddly therapeutic to go all around the house with a sponge and a spray bottle and clean off the windowsills, relishing every smear of soot I wipe up, knowing some of it is probably several months old.

But not very often.

Most of the time, I'm happier operating more like my husband's been operating all along, as a slacker wife. Almost any day, I'd rather be out throwing a baseball or building a snowman with Belle and Joe than going around the house with a sponge. And then I'd rather come in late and heat up a frozen entree than have to start mincing the shallots two hours before dinner time. And then afterwards I'd rather flop into bed, too tired from running after ground balls to even brush my hair, much less put on a mud masque.

I do want to make things nice for my children and my husband, but I've calculated that each one of us will get more out of the snowman than the shallots, both in the short run and the long. We can have a nice dinner conversation over chicken pot pies and a salad just as well as we can have one over an herbed rack of lamb.

I know that my fathers, my brothers, and I survived quite well on Swanson's when we had to. When my mother was on the haying crew, for instance.

I remember her coming in late from the fields during the summer, when I was growing up, her hair full of hay seed and her nostrils full of dust. Her job during haying season was driving the winch—a pickup truck that didn't go anywhere. My father had disconnected the drive shaft to power the two steel drums that spooled the cables that ran the pole basket up and down the beaver slide, dumping loads of hay into the portable stack yard. The basket sat at the bottom of the slide waiting for the buck rakes to come and unload their piles of loose hay, which they did about every twenty seconds. Then my mother would put the winch in gear, picking up the slack in the cables, and give her the gas, causing the steel drums to wind the cable and hoist the 15-foot basket up the slide. As the cables whipped through the pulleys at the top of the slide, the basket ran up the 45-degree wooden slats, slowly or lickety split, depending on precisely where my mother intended to place the load of hay.

She made it look easy but it wasn't, and very few people did it well. If you ran the basket up too fast, you could break the top pulleys right off the slide and kill someone with the falling basket. One of our ranch hands did that one time, although he didn't kill any of the stackers; he was lucky enough to merely break somebody's arm. If you let it back down without braking at the exact right moment, the cables could snap at the bottom and the basket would go flying out into the meadow. And your timing with the clutch made all the difference in how quickly or slowly the hay dropped out of the basket onto the top of the stack, and how much area you covered.

My mother's finesse with this crude piece of cobbled-together machinery lessened the workload for the four hands with pitchforks who were standing inside the stack yard itself, filling the corners. It also meant that stacking progressed quickly. Our old-fashioned loose stacks held about 20 tons of hay and on a good long summer day this crew could put up half a dozen of them—120 tons in all.

In July and August I was on the hay crew myself, driving a tractor with a side delivery rake. But in September I had to go back to school. After I got home from school on those afternoons, I would always run out to wherever they'd moved the stack yard and watch the work, and I remember so clearly the way my mother muscled the gearshift and revved the accelerator, the fragments of conversation we'd have between loads as I got her caught up on my school day.

I can also recall, with no effort, the way she branded calves as efficiently and humanely as possible, without flinching, and the way she rode her horse, also without flinching, straight into the high spring rapids of Crystal Creek after a gallivanting heifer.

I remember the way she coaxed a nervous cow into the stall and physically helped it through a difficult delivery, and the way this 110-pound woman could somehow heave a cumbersome saddle onto her horse without letting it thud down onto his back. I can picture her driving her snowmobile up the ranch road too, red-cheeked, squint-eyed, and hell bent for leather, with me holding on for dear life to her waist.

I don't remember her cooking that well.

We ate quite a bit of beef, I know, but other than stuffed heart, which was a specialty, the details aren't coming back to me. Somehow there was always a meal on the table, I'm pretty sure of that. We were well-enough fed. But she didn't try to be too creative and she was always on a budget, with her time as well as with her money.

I don't remember my mom doing a lot of housecleaning, and in the only way I can picture it in my mind's eye, she's in a hurry. But I also don't remember that our house was dirty. Perhaps it was.

I don't remember that my mom ever had a mud masque on her face.

I don't remember her ever trying to get my father to vacuum, either. I don't know, maybe my father should have done more vacuuming. But I don't think clean carpets were a real high priority in our house for either one of them, especially during the summer.

I've know I've spent a lot of time in this book talking about how we modern-day wives have too much to do, and I know I'm not the first person to point that out. But it seems like the debate I hear revolves, most of the time, around how to get the men in our lives to pick up more of the household duties.

I would never say we shouldn't address that, because I agree that a lot of men could do a better job of pitching in on the domestic front, including my own husband. But I don't think that would solve the most important problem that we modern-day wives, stretched to the breaking point, have.

I think our biggest problem is that just being a wife itself is now subject to standards of perfection and levels of performance that are unrealistic and unnecessary. This just doesn't seem like progress, really, for our gender. This seems like a change for the worse, not for the better. Domestic duties were a necessary undertaking for my mother, but that wasn't what life was all about. Those things took place in the background of her life, not the foreground.

207

I find it very strange that these things seem more important for my generation of wives than they did for hers.

My mother and grandmother weren't expected to rid their households of every molecule of bacteria and speck of dust. They weren't expected to know how to prepare dishes being served in some gourmet restaurant in some far-flung climate, and it was okay to have a limited repertoire. They weren't expected to look half their actual age. They weren't expected to launder everyone else's clothes after just one wearing. And they weren't expected to be supermoms creating superkids.

How did this happen to our generation, I wonder? It seems like the standards of homemaking and child rearing started to get absurdly high about the same time women began *leaving* their homes to enter the workforce. So ironically, the less time we have to get all this stuff done, the more we are expected to do.

The bar on cooking, for instance, seems to essentially be set at a professional level. Professional appliances, professional cookware, and professional recipes are practically the norm. Cleaning is even more ridiculous, because it's no longer enough to make the beds and pick up the clutter—we've now been convinced that everything in our world is infected and must be disinfected. And smell like perfume too. The cleanser section at the supermarket is one of the largest in the store, and I'm sure personal grooming products aren't far behind. And entertaining has become so professionalized and so competitive in some neighborhoods that it's not even fun any more.

You might expect me to blame women's magazines and television shows for this. And yes, I think that the magazines and TV shows—and especially their advertisers—do set very high standards for how our houses are supposed to be decorated, what kinds of dishes we're supposed to be serving, and most problematic, how we ourselves are supposed to look.

But I don't think the magazines and television shows would be in business if we weren't tuning in by the millions. And I'm sure their advertisers wouldn't continue to support them if we weren't spending our money on the stuff they're advertising by the billions.

I don't think we can blame the men in our lives either, as convenient and popular as that might be. My husband might be a slacker himself when it comes to housekeeping, but he doesn't tell me what to do. He doesn't tell me how to spend the money I earn, or who to vote for, or much less that I could certainly find a better way of removing soap scum if I would only try.

I'm afraid that the only person I can blame for the times I've gotten caught up in the pursuit of domestic perfection is myself.

Maybe that's not too surprising, though. Maybe it's women exactly like myself, those who've had a career at some point or are in the middle of one, who are usually the ones overdoing it on the domestic front. It's ironic, but perhaps women like myself are trying to bring the same aggressive and competitive zeal to our domestic pursuits that we bring to our careers. So even though we don't have time to operate at the June Cleaver level, we might well be the ones responsible for raising the standards far beyond those that June Cleaver or even our own mothers were ever expected to meet.

So maybe now that we've managed to such a great extent to liberate ourselves from men, we need to liberate ourselves from ourselves.

One time a well-meaning acquaintance gave me a very attractive little book on how to fold napkins. In retrospect I'm disappointed in the way I initially reacted to this book. I'm an inherently competitive person, and just looking at the book's cover gave me the sudden feeling that I was a bumpkin in this particular field. This book was written by a true napkin folding expert—for the enlightenment of housewives, not restaurateurs. It made me realize that napkin folding was just another womanly skill which I might have thought I possessed (to whatever minimal extent it was necessary), but which in fact I had never properly learned, much less performed at its zenith.

I came to my senses quickly, at least. I snapped out of my napkin delirium after just a few moments. But it's an example of how easy it is to feel inadequate when you see books or television shows or magazines articles that demonstrate how you, too, can perform like a pro with wifely pursuits such as napkin folding. Suddenly you think you've got to get with the program—that you're actually supposed to be doing these things. Never mind that so many of these pursuits are ultimately inconsequential; we can still work on perfecting our skills.

Our country seems to be in love with experts on practically every subject, though, no matter how mundane or how long we might have been doing these things without the advice of a specialist. Just go to the self-help section of the bookstore and you'll see that we can now be given instructions on how to properly do such things as talk to our dogs . . . get dressed for our jobs . . . live simply . . . arrange our furniture . . . play with our toddlers . . . have sex . . . drink wine . . . go on a date . . . hang clothes in our closets . . . go for a walk . . . even sleep in our beds.

These instruction books have now been published, for our edification, on thousands of subjects. Many of them say right in their titles that they're for "dummies" or "idiots," and this is not insulting to us readers, eerily; it's actually an effective marketing ploy. Apparently we've come to believe that we are dullards indeed, and we are buying these books by the handfuls.

I don't believe I'm an idiot, though, in spite of the fact that I never read the napkin-folding book and remain thoroughly uninformed on the subject. It just doesn't have any significance for me, to tell you the truth.

211

I think about how I remember my mother, the kinds of challenging enterprises I remember her pouring herself into, and my fond hope is that when Belle and Joe look back at their childhood, they'll have similar recollections of me.

"My mother could fold a napkin to look like a flamingo" is not how I hope Belle will begin her own memoir.

Frankly, I don't want my husband to think that's the kind of contribution he can expect from me either.

I don't believe that the viability of my relationship with my husband is a function of whether or not his dinner is always on the table when he gets home, anyway, much less how his napkin might be folded. I know that the strength of our bond isn't a function of whether or not my hair is always perfectly coifed. And I know it's not a function of whether or not our windowsills are covered with dust, or clean. I believe it's a function of the love and respect we have for each other as equals in our marriage and in our lives.

I am aware that there are books out there that tell you that if you'll just be a good wife and make your husband happy, you'll be happy yourself. If you'll just make sure he has a good square meal set down in front of him. If you'll just make sure you're packing his children off to plenty of scheduled play dates and enriching activities. If you'll just make sure he gets the sexual satisfaction he desires according to the schedule he wishes. If you'll just make sure he never runs out of clean underwear.

But why? So he can worry about more important things? I believe I have more important things to worry about myself. And that's not the kind of woman I aspire to be, even if it would make my husband happy.

Besides, I never wanted to strike that kind of bargain with a man, where I serve him so that he can be happy and be nice to me and the kids. I would hope that formula is passé for every woman as far as marriage is concerned, whether she is home rearing the children or out earning the rent money.

But I don't really think my husband needs or wants a female servant anyway. From what I know of the man, he wants the same thing I want. An emotional, physical, and intellectual connection to a partner he respects. My husband might get less out of me as far as cooking and cleaning than he might have expected he'd get from a wife, but we do have a really great time together. If he just wanted someone to wash his socks, he could take them over to the drop-bundle laundry.

I do wash his socks, though. He seems to still respect me. He washes my car, and I still respect him. We both know a certain amount of menial drudgery, along with a logical division of labor, is necessary in life. But he has so many more important things to contribute to my life than car washing. And I hope he'd say the same thing about me.

He seems to love me, even though my hair is usually a mess. Even though our house is full of germs. Even though our dinner guests have to eat store-bought pies. And even though our children think unloading the dishwasher is their job, not mine.

And I love him, too. He might be a slacker, a sluggard, and a slouch, but what can I say? We're in the same camp.